THE FLIP OF A COIN

Tommy Allsup (1999)

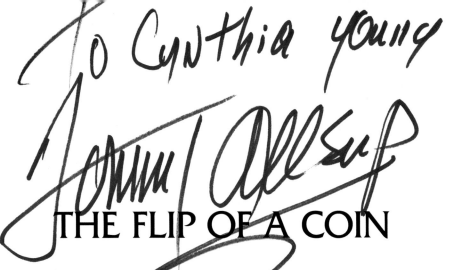

To Cynthia Young

Tommy Allsup

THE FLIP OF A COIN

The story of Tommy Allsup with Buddy Holly,
Bob Wills and other music legends

Guy Logsdon

Guy Logsdon Books

First Edition

Published by Guy Logsdon Books
PO Box 520982
Tulsa OK 74152-0982
Designed by Bill Patterson

ISBN 978-0-615-42909-0

Printed in the United States

DEDICATION

First I dedicate this book to my children: to my daughters Gayla, Robin and Annie and to my sons Tommy, Jr. and Austin – I love you all!

And I'd like to make a special dedication to my wife, Nicole. She's a great inspiration to me; she has the kindest, most open heart and has taught me the true meaning of love. She also happens to be the best cook in the world! I'll love you eternally, sweetheart.

Last and certainly not least, TO ALL OF MY BUDDY HOLLY AND BOB WILLS FANS; I've tried to keep their music alive all these years. I thank you all for helping me do so. God bless you all, and enjoy the book.

CONTENTS

FOREWORD

As 1931 drew to a close, the turmoil of the '30s was in full swing. Japanese troops launched attacks in Manchuria as an early step in their plans to invade and occupy China. In Spain King Alfonso abdicated as political turmoil set the stage for an all out civil war. In Germany over five million people were unemployed; their economy collapsed and their banks were closed, thus allowing Hitler and the Nazi Party to gain popularity and power. In the United States the Great Depression was eating deeper into the pockets of the nation, so to stimulate pride and patriotism on March 3, 1931 the "Star Spangled Banner" was declared our national anthem. The Southern and Midwestern states that had enjoyed cotton as the king of agriculture were suffering from international competition that provided a higher grade of cotton – thus placing sharecropper and tenant farmers into a migrant pool of displaced workers. In Oklahoma, the Panhandle counties along with the contiguous states were experiencing the early stages of drought that continued through the decade creating the "Dust Bowl" image. In rural eastern Oklahoma there was no drought problem, and farmers continued to grow subsistence crops for family consumption; the Great Depression was having marginal effect on rural Oklahoma life styles because most of those families already knew how to do without the luxuries of life – they had never known any luxuries. Also, many of the families were of American Indian descent and had received their land - debt free - prior to statehood; if they owed money, it was probably for seed, not for the land. During this growing worldwide turmoil, on Tuesday, November 24, 1931 two days before Thanksgiving on an eighty acre farm near Owasso, Oklahoma, Tommy Douglas Allsup was born, the twelfth of thirteen children, to Thomas Jerry and Retta M. (Blakemore) Allsup; Tommy's mother was of Cherokee Indian descent (Dawes Commission Enrollment #8301).

In the early nineteenth century as the nation grew the demand for land that was owned by various Indian tribes, particularly in the South, was being encroached on and often stolen by white settlers. Land now known as Oklahoma was set aside to be the home of American Indians removed from their lands; it was designated "Indian Territory". As American Indians were forcibly driven from their homes and land, there were "Trails of Tears" that took them to Indian Territory. The one to receive more attention historically was the Cherokee Trail of Tears. Tommy Allsup's great-grandmother walked that trail. Later, when the Civil War was waged, Indian nations in Indian Territory were divided in loyalties – Cherokee fought Cherokee; therefore, when the hostilities ended, new treaties and division of lands were forced on the tribes by the government, and the central part of the Indian Territory became the "Unassigned Lands" – no American Indians were placed there. As demand for the Indian lands continued to grow, the government decided that the "Unassigned Lands" should be opened to settlement in 1889 by a land run. That massive migration for free land was followed by other land runs for acreage declared to be public lands taken from various Indian tribes; western Indian Territory was renamed "Oklahoma Territory". The Twin Territories - Indian Territory and Oklahoma Territory - were governed by different laws with Indian Territory divided into sovereign Indian nations, and all land in Indian Territory was owned in common by each Indian nation.

Statehood became a wide spread movement in Oklahoma Territory, but Indian leaders did not want to relinquish American Indian self-determination. Therefore, Indian Territory leaders organized "The State of Sequoyah" with a well written constitution, but Congress rejected an all Indian state and decided that both territories would be admitted as the State of Oklahoma. Before statehood in November 1907, all Indians in the territories were to be enrolled in the appropriate tribe or nation and deeded land. The amount of acreage was determined by the amount of "Indian blood". Among the Five Civilized Tribes – Cherokee, Choctaw, Chickasaw, Creek, and Seminole – the enrollment was handled by the Dawes Commission. Retta Maudine Blakemore was enrolled as a nine (9) year old Cherokee female, one-fourth (1/4) blood, census card number 3396, enrollment number 8301, page 289 in the Dawes Final Rolls. As a quarter blood Cherokee she was deeded eighty acres of land. However, Tommy's family always believed that she was more than a quarter blood, for at that time in Oklahoma history many American Indians believed that it was a disadvantage to be Indian and claimed to be less than they were. His grandmother may have been a full blood Cherokee.

The Allsups came from England in the early 1800s, and a group of them eventually settled in Marion County, Illinois where Tommy's father, Thomas Jerry Allsup, was born in 1880. By 1890, when his father's family moved to the Cherokee Nation, the laws had changed to allow non-Indians to lease land and farm in the Nation. They settled west of Claremore on the Verdigris River about four miles down the river from the old Will Rogers Home Place. Family stories relate that Will Rogers and their Uncle Bob, as young boys, often played together. Their father remembered seeing Will around the Allsup place when they were young.

Tommy's Uncle John Allsup, one of the early family arrivals in the area, had a pool hall in the Owasso settlement in the early 1890s; a little later he moved to Tulsa, where the family believes he had the first pool hall in Tulsa. According to Tommy he bootlegged and ran a pool hall on Main Street. In the 1890s in Tulsa, Main Street was just a road with mostly wooden buildings on each side. Tommy recalled, "Dad said that he and Uncle Bob liked to watch Uncle John count his money; they would look around the corner and watch – he had two big pearl handled forty-fives and would put them up on the bar and pour his money out on the bar and count it". Tommy also recounted that his mother's first cousin was Buffalo Bill Cody; her grandmother was a Cody. She often told her children that she was related to Buffalo Bill.

Retta Blakemore's allotted eighty acres were approximately two miles west of Owasso, Oklahoma, at that time a small settlement eight miles northeast of Tulsa; it derived its name from an Osage Indian word that means "the end", for it was the terminus for a branch of the Santa Fe Railway. Her land was farm land with no house until she and her husband had the resources to build a home on it a few years after they started rearing a family, a family of thirteen children: Bill, the oldest was born March 8, 1910; followed by Lorene, June 15, 1912; Leta, January 14, 1914; Laverne, December 8, 1916; Mildred, March 16, 1918; Odell, March 15, 1919; Gladys, December 29, 1920; Joe, November 27, 1923; Marcella, April 17, 1925; Buel "Chico", February 5, 1926; Kenneth, November 19, 1928; Tommy, November 24, 1931; and Della Darlene, February 28, 1939.

INTRODUCTION

It was cold! Cold!! COLD!!! It was a miserably cold tour that started in Chicago and daily became more unbearable as the entertainers wound their way through northern states. It ended for three of the musicians who were trying to escape the cold on a day designated by some fans as *"the day the music died"*. Following their concert in Clear Lake, Iowa in the early hours of 3 February 1959, Buddy Holly, Ritchie Valens and J. P. Richardson, better known as "The Big Bopper", were killed, when for unknown reasons their Beechcraft plane crashed. But for the flip of a coin it would have been Tommy Allsup, who was The Crickets guitarist and who is currently a highly respected guitarist, bass guitarist, western swing band leader and award winning guitarist and record producer, instead of Ritchie Valens. Much has been written about that tour and fatal evening, but this is Tommy Allsup's story that started on a farm in northeastern Oklahoma and carried him through his own high school band, a member of the legendary Johnnie Lee Wills band, his own bands in Oklahoma, Texas, and New Mexico, a friend of Buddy Holly and a Cricket, producer of Bob Wills, Willie Nelson, and other major recordings and a Grammy Award winning guitarist. He is a dedicated western swing musician who believes that music is categorized by how you play the song. Tommy said that Fred Rose was writing country songs for Hank Williams, but *"he wrote 'Roly Poly' and it became a western swing song. What if Bob hadn't cut it and Roy Acuff did; what kind of song would it have been? If Bob put them out first, they were considered to be western swing songs. A good song is a good song, and I have no problem making it swing or making it a 2 / 4 commercial Nashville song; it's how you play it"*.

The following pages reflect how Tommy Allsup has played music and life, and his story is told in first person through the rest of this narrative. *Information by others will be italicized.*

Chapter 1
THE EARLY DAYS

I guess my dad and mother only had three addresses in their married lives. When they got married, they lived about a half mile west of where she got her Indian land, on her brother's land. He must have gotten his first; then they moved east of there, and later to Claremore. Six of my brothers and sisters were born on the place that belonged to my Uncle Smokey; seven of us were born at the place that was my mother's allotment.

Tommy and his sister Darlene eating watermelon, circa 1939.

Our water wells – one in the pasture and one near the house – were deep. They had been gas wells, and it was sulphur water. All of us kids were raised on sulphur water; you can't get near it. It stinks worse than rotten eggs, but we've been pretty healthy all our lives. That water may have helped. We pumped it into the horse troughs and the minerals would collect at the bottom – we had to clean it out three or four times each year. The places around us didn't have that sulphur; it was strange. Our well flowed all the time down in the pasture, so we always had a little creek. During harvest we would help our neighbors and they would come over and help us. None of us had money to hire help, so we helped one another. Our horses and livestock would drink out of that creek and

1

the troughs, but the neighbors horses wouldn't drink our sulphur water. We did have a pond down in the pasture where they would go drink. It's pretty bad when animals won't drink it, but men will. My sister Mildred and I were by the old home place a few years ago, and the house is about to fall in. Our folks had capped off a well near the house and put a pump on it and ran a pipe up to the yard with a faucet on it. Mildred turned it on and ran twenty feet away; the odor was so bad. She said, "Did we used to drink that stuff"? I said, "Yeh! All our lives". When we lived there we let it run for a minute or two, and it got ice cold. We had a little shower set up

"This picture is of me is in 1943 when I was 12 years old; I'm playing a C chord. That was right after we left Owasso and were in Claremore. The younger musician is one of my nephews, David Allsup".

down in the pasture; we took an old gas tank out of a car, hung a bucket under it, and punched holes in it. My brothers ran pipes up to the well so we could fill the tank. It was ice cold and great in the summer time where we could run down and cool off.

Our house was a bedroom, a living room, and a kitchen. The bedroom had two double beds, and the living room had a double bed and a couch. Four boys could sleep in one bed – two at one end, two at the other end. People wouldn't think of doing that now. In the summer time, we didn't sleep in the house; we made a pallet outside and slept there. In those days, you could take your mattress down to the barn and put straw

2

in it and place it anywhere, and think nothing about it. It was almost a square house with a pretty good size back porch where we kept a cream separator. We separated cream from the milk and sold the milk. We put it in cans and stored it in cold water. A man came by each morning to pick it up and take it to Tulsa. We sold milk and cream. Daddy always had fifteen to sixteen milk cows. There would always be two or three ten gallon cans of milk there. It took a lot of milk for a family that size, and we also made our own butter. Of course we canned vegetables in the summer. My older brothers worked over at the Halsell Ranch (*a legendary ranch between Claremore and Vinita, Oklahoma*). My brother Chico spent nearly his whole life there, as well as the ranch up at Lenapah.

My brother Bill was the first to leave home, but I remember when there were four boys and two girls who caught the school bus to get to Owasso and school. One time my brothers got me to stick my tongue to the mail box one cold morning, and it stuck. I got to do all the dirty work because I was the youngest boy. My brothers Kenneth and Chico were just older than me and had me do all the dirty work, and I got all the whippings for it. But we have always been a close family; there have never been any fallings out. Nobody ever stays mad over ten minutes, and there are some 150 nieces and nephews. Anytime we got together or get together, there's music.

Tommy's sister, Marcie, and a friend Doris Fry, with their Owasso house in the background.

We used to go to town to get ice, roll it in newspapers and

put in tow sacks; we'd get home and break it up with the side of an ax to make ice cream – never heard of crushed ice. We were so far out in the country that the only thing we got delivered was the mail. We went to school in Owasso; I was there for six years. They ran six school busses; Owasso wasn't very big in those days.

My daddy was a fiddle player and my oldest brother, Bill, was a guitar player. He's the one who bought a Gibson guitar for $35 back in the '30s. My brother, Odell, played the guitar, and Kenneth played the guitar. Only one brother, Chico, couldn't play anything. All my sisters sang pretty good, but they didn't play instruments. We always had music around the house. My daddy probably fiddled every day of his life; he was an old breakdown fiddler. That's how I started, playing square dances with him.

I also learned to play the fiddle; not only was my dad a fiddler, my brother Bill was a pretty good breakdown fiddler. When we lived near Owasso, we had an old fiddle that only had one string on it – the A string. I learned to play the melody on one string. My brother Kenneth would hit me a chord, and I would tune that string to the chord of C or D. The first song I learned was "There's an Old Apple Tree in the Orchard" on that one string. I worried my brother to death to second me on that tune. We sold a cow or something and finally got enough money to buy some more strings, and I learned some breakdowns. We always had a guitar, mandolin, and fiddle around the house. Oreon Yates who taught me a lot on the guitar after we moved to Claremore had a brother, Bucky Yates, who was a good fiddler, and sometimes I would fiddle with them.

I was probably 10 years old when we played our first dance and got paid for it. Doc Glass was the head doctor at Saint Johns Hospital. He would have a party every year for the doctors, nurses, and staff at St. Johns. He lived a mile north and two miles east of Owasso, and had a

4

big house with twenty-eight rooms and a big barn. His daughter raised Arabian horses. We went to his house and played that night. A man who worked for him named Raymond came and picked up my dad and me. Dad didn't have a car; when we went to town, we traveled in a wagon. Doc Glass had a big library; I remember he had a room with a marble floor where they danced, book shelves all the way around it – leather furniture. There was a kitchen with big refrigerators. At that time we only had an ice box – put a block of ice in it to keep a few things cool. I was impressed by his house. On this big table he had beer and cheese shipped in from every where. He would talk these nurses and folks through a square dance; they'd practice a few minutes. Then we would play a break down and they would square dance. Then he would show them how to waltz. When it was over we were paid maybe $6 or $7 a piece. I was out chopping corn for a dollar a day; in the hay field you got a penny a bale. If you got a job on a dairy in the summer you couldn't make over $30 a month, and you had to milk 30 or 40 cows. To make $6 for a few hours of playing music made you feel rich.

My brother Bill probably taught me a couple of chords, at least enough to play those hoedowns. When we moved to Claremore in 1942, Oreon Yates lived around the corner from us. He was a good fiddle player and a good guitar player, and he had a lot of good swing records. When I was about fifteen years old, I used to go around there to pick his brain. He worked in Tulsa, and not long ago, he told me that he would come home and say "I sure hope Tommy doesn't come over wanting to play; I sure am tired, and about that time you would show up with that old guitar".

I started playing guitar for him, and we would go up in those Dog Creek Hills and play for the Indians. Claremore had two creeks; the west side was Cat Creek and the east side was Dog Creek – it came out of the Claremore Lake. So they called the hills around old Highway 66 near Foyil and Chelsea the Dog Creek Hills at least they did when I was a kid. One time some Indians wanted us to play, and Oreon and I said, "Okay, but we're getting out of there if you start fightin', an' you've got to pass the hat before we play and you get drunk". The man who was hiring us was a short Cherokee Indian named Alf Naves; he was married to somebody who was kin to us. So he passed the hat and put the money which was mostly change in a sack, and Oreon put it in his fiddle case. I hadn't even taken my guitar out of the case; they had already moved all of the furniture out of the house into the yard.

At house dances we would sit in the door way between the bedroom and living room where they danced. Well, they were full of moonshine, and one hell of a fight started. Oreon said, "Come on Tommy, we're going". He had a model A Ford; we jumped in it, went down the hill toward home. When we got there, we had $26; he said, "They knew if they fought, we were going' ta leave". Actually, we had $13.41 each; Oreon figured it to the penny. The other side of the story is that if Oreon got too much moonshine, he would say, "Tommy, there's the speedometer now don't let me get over 30". He had to watch the road – they weren't lighted in those days, and sometimes I had to use a flashlight. Oreon would drink, but he didn't like fights.

Tommy's dad and Bob Bone butchering a hog in 1940 that weighed over 600 pounds. "My brother, Joe, had an old stag and sow that were huge; they were his Future Farmers of America project".

6

In Claremore, we stayed at my aunt's house until my dad could sell his livestock and farm equipment. Then he bought a house that had two bedrooms. Our address in Claremore was 1201 West Strain, near the Will Rogers Memorial. Our first house had one bedroom and a path (to the outhouse); our second one had two bedrooms and a bath. When I was twelve years old, I had running water. My dad was 52 when I was born, and was 85 when he died. He was buried out west of Claremore along the Verdigris River where they settled when they came down in 1890 from Marion County, Illinois.

Tommy's father, Thomas Jerry Allsup, photographed in the late 1950s

Tommy's sister, Darlene, recalled that Tommy and she were the youngest and probably were spoiled, also, "He's eight years older than I, so he was too old to be a playmate but young enough to be a 'pest.' One of our neighbors said she always knew when he was chasing me around the house with a dead mouse because she could hear me screaming. He loved to sit around and pick on his guitar, and sometimes that interfered with Mama and my radio programs. I'd tell Mama, 'Make him quit that noise'. Glad she didn't pay attention to me". Tommy recalled that he was always pulling tricks on her like putting grasshoppers in her hair.

At a family gathering in 1997, his sister Laverne, the third sibling in the family, related that she could not tell all that she knew about him, for

7

some things should not be told. Indeed, the Allsup family enjoyed only one luxury of rural Oklahoma life – they learned to love and respect one another, not material things. It is a luxury that the entire family shares and enjoys.

Laverne did not say that shoes were so new to him that he put them on backwards; instead, she recalled that they were size five, black patent leather with white shoe strings – "he wasn't a year old, he was just a big ol' boy"! She continued, "We picked cotton; that's one thing our mother taught us to do. We shared what we had with the other kids, because there were so many of us that we had to. Actually, he was just a little spoiled brat because of the rest of us; we always called him Tommy Doug until he left and went out on his on. Then he chose to be called what ever

he wanted people to call him. Actually, he was a good ol' kid considering the shape he was in – he was a good kid". Another family member said that he didn't do his work because, "Babies don't work"! Tommy recalled that he did his fair share, particularly when the mules were tired.

When they moved to Claremore, their father would work at the Will Rogers Memorial. The family recalled that: "People would think that he was related to Will Rogers

"This is a picture made in 1910 of my dad and a cowboy named Lige Hopkins, they're wearing chaps. I had a photographer superimpose me in the middle and used this photo on a guitar instrumental album of Charley Pride hits that we did in 1969. You can barely see my guitar in the background".

8

The Allsup family, on the ground Mildred and Darlene; seated l. to r. Lorene, Laverne, Daddy, Momma, Gladys, Marcie; standing l. to r., Bill, Odie, Joe, Buel, Kenneth, Tommy; 1952.

because he knew him as a young man. Our mother's grandmother was 'Aunt Sara,' a mid-wife to his mother when Will Rogers was born; she was also a wet nurse to some of the other Rogers kids". The family memory relates that in approximately 1901 a young man came riding up to the Allsup place and asked to sleep in the barn for the night; they let him, and the next morning someone asked who that Indian kid was and they replied that he said that he was Cherokee Jack – a name used by Will Rogers. The family legend says that on another occasion the young Will Rogers came by their house barefooted with spurs on. Laverne and others remembered that when their grandmother Allsup died, "There were so many of us; we loaded up in cars and Tommy was going to walk. He and his cousin, my son, stopped to buy a Coke – they missed the funeral for a soft drink"!

My sister Marcie was married in 1941, and lived a quarter of a mile up the pasture. A couple of days after they were married – they lived behind their in-laws – I was up there and it was storming. They said, "You'll have to spend the night". So I went out and slept with her and her new husband – they only had one bed. My real problem according to my sister was that I would bring my dog with me. My dog was a registered "Mutt" – a pure bred mutt; we always had dogs. We always had horses, but we couldn't ride our work horses. We rode the cows if we thought our folks wouldn't catch us. My mother and daddy married in 1910; she was seventeen, and they had thirteen kids. They started off going to the Nazarene Church in Owasso, but when we moved to Claremore they switched over to the Baptist Church. You know, Baptists were liberal compared to Nazarenes when I was growing up. A monsignor told me once in Fort Worth before a ball game – they were going to do this Cowboy football game – and he had this little drink with him – the Coors Distributor had a big box, and he said, "You know, we Catholics aren't the only ones who drink; if you see four Baptists together, you'll see a fifth near by".

When Tommy was growing up and playing dances in Oklahoma, it was a dry state; prohibition was the watch word that protected morality. Only beer that was 3.2 could be sold; to most who drank, it was dish water. To those who did not drink, it was the devil in a beer bottle. The other great sin was dancing; however, like Texas, Oklahoma was a dancing state. Dance halls and American Legion halls, where many dances were held, dotted the country side; Oklahoma danced all Saturday night, and prayed all Sunday morning. In 1943, in order to protect its citizenry, the state legislators, some slightly inebriated when the vote was taken, passed laws that prohibited selling or drinking beer where dancing was allowed. Beer could not be sold and dance halls could not be operated near churches or schools. Since there was no liquor to be sold or consumed in a dance hall, there was no age limit on who could enter and dance or watch and listen. Entire families attended dances played by Bob Wills and His Texas Playboys. Often they did not dance – they were there to hear the music and meet the musicians. This love of western swing music and family attendance was extended to include Johnnie Lee Wills and All His Boys, Leon McAuliffe and His Cimarron Boys, Hank Thompson and His Brazos Valley Boys, and numerous locally popular bands. Anyone of any age from cradle to grave could attend a dance if they had the money for admission.

In Tulsa, the legendary Cain's Ballroom was the popular western swing dance hall. It is where Bob Wills gained his fame and popularity, and when he left Tulsa for California in the summer of 1942, he made his brother Johnnie Lee Wills and All His Boys take over the Cain's dances and noon day radio broadcasts over KVOO Radio. O. W. Mayo, who was Bob and Johnnie Lee Wills' manager, purchased Cain's and continued the strong western swing tradition until the 1970s. The guitarist who had the greatest influence on creating the Wills/Texas Playboy sound was Eldon Shamblin; he developed the moving rhythm chord progression that became the standard rhythm guitar style. Others followed such as Junior Bernard, Ebb Gray, Don Tolle, and Tommy Allsup.

When I got to be about sixteen I was tall enough to get in Cain's, and I would go watch Eldon Shamblin when he was in town and Ebb Gray who played with Johnnie Lee, and all those guys. But Oreon taught me a lot and got me started on the swing stuff. He taught me to chop off the chords and got me started right on playing rhythm.

In 1947 when I was a sophomore in high school we started a little band called the Oklahoma Swing Billies. We had it for about a year. We'd play the American Legion halls in Collinsville and Chelsea, but we had a regular Saturday night at Claremore. We used to pack them with dancers, which was good. When I started playing with them, I learned to play a little lead guitar, but mostly I played rhythm guitar. That's what I had originally learned to play, and one of my friends thought that I was better than I really was.

Archie Bingham and I were buddies in high school, and he and I had gone to see Ray Reed and the Cross B Boys. They were there with Bob Crosby, the legendary rodeo cowboy from New Mexico, for the annual Will Rogers Rodeo in Claremore. Ray had a big western swing band that traveled in a huge truck. Bob Crosby carried his horses in it, and the band had living quarters in the front. Ray later told me that they had practiced for six months before going on the road. The band included two fiddles, trumpet, accordion, two guitars, drums, bass, and steel guitar. It was a big band, but one of the guitarists, who was from Clovis, New Mexico was returning to Clovis to work in the Norman Petty Trio. Ray needed another guitar player.

Well, the next night Archie came by the house and said, "Get your guitar and amp and come down to the dance; they're waitin' to hear you play". The guitarists had big beautiful cut-away Epiphone guitars and big amplifiers, and I had a little ol' Gibson with a DeArmand pickup and an amp the size of a Post Toasties box. Now I had no idea what Archie was talking about when he said that they were waiting to hear me play. So we go down to the dance with Archie carrying my amp and me the guitar. We get there and the guitar players were sitting there, and had me set up. The steel player said, "Boy, can you play the third part to 'Hang Your

The Oklahoma Swing Billies in late 1947: Jay Bushyhead, bass; Oreon Yates, fiddle; Tommy Allsup, guitar; Pat Johnson, drums; Neal Vest, sax; Alfred Litchenberg, steel guitar.

Tommy Allsup and His Range Riders bus, Will Rogers Day, 1949, Claremore, Oklahoma. "I was right behind Bob Wills and his new $16,000 bus. The motor was up front; we had no heater, so at night we would raise the hood a little to heat the bus. This is the one on which we used a pipe for a muffler; you could hear it coming for miles. It was the only vehicle I owned until I went to work for Johnnie Lee Wills in 1952".

Head in Shame'"? I said, "I can't even play the lead". He said, "You're
probably too young to go on the road with us anyway". I was only sixteen.
My good friend Archie Bingham had set it up for me, but didn't realize
that they were a step or two above me. However, Ray Reed and I stayed in
contact for the next fifty years, and often worked together at the Lincoln
County Symposium in New Mexico. Ray was quite a man.

When I was a senior, I thought, "Well, I think I want my own band".
I got a young steel guitar player, a year younger than I, named Bill Roy,
I said, "Let's get our own band". So we did – Tommy Allsup and His
Range Riders. I don't remember why we were the Range Riders; maybe
we saw it in a cowboy movie. It was Paul McGhee who came up with the
idea. The Range Riders were Paul on drums, Bill Roy on the steel guitar,
Willard Chambers on the fiddle, and me playing the guitar. We got the
Clugston brothers from Tulsa and Billy Markel to join us. I had met Bill
Roy in high school, while he was taking steel guitar lessons in Tulsa.
He had a little single neck steel, and was a fast learner. He and I worked
together off and on for many years.

*Tommy's sister Darlene recalled, "When he first started out with his
band, we had musical instruments all over the house. The band would
rehearse under a shade tree in the summer, so in order for them to have
the words of a song, I would start and stop a record until I had all the
words copied off for them. Guess he couldn't afford sheet music. When
he had been out either playing or just jamming, whenever he came in,
any time of the night, Mama would get up and fix biscuits and gravy for
him and whomever was with him. When I went to my first day of Algebra
Class, my freshman year, the teacher asked me if I was kin to Tommy. I
told her he was my brother, and she informed me that if I was as ornery*

as he was, I was in for trouble. She said there were days when she wanted to hang him out the window".

In those days, they had musicals at peoples' homes. As I learned more chords, we would come down to Tulsa and do radio shows. I remember they had the Avery Coliseum in Tulsa, and the Clugston Brothers had a Saturday radio show; we would come down and be on it and often play their dances. When I started the Range Riders, I used Roy Clugston who was a bass player – he worked at a funeral home out at Sand Springs. He would tell me and Bill Roy, "Why don't you get your guitars and come over and we'll play – practice some songs". He would want to get back there where the bodies were and practice songs; we were just kids, and it was kind of spooky. I said, "Doesn't this brother you"? He said, "Naw, they're not gonna hurt you". He had to be there as the night man, but it was weird. If we practiced, that's where we had to practice.

Leon McAuliffe had purchased a new bus in the latter part of 1948. He put his old bus on a car lot to sell. We bought it, but we were too young to get credit. Our fiddle player, Willard Chambers was a mechanic for one of the car dealers and a little older than us, so he signed a note for $500 dollars – we bought a bus. Now it takes $500,000 to buy one. It was an old Flex that Leon had worn out; I think Leon might have gotten it from Bob Wills – one of Bob's early busses. We got the bus, and there was a man in Claremore who was a real good mechanic. We said, "Do you want to be our bus driver; if you do, you have to keep the bus running". He said, "The first thing, let's take the muffler off". That make of bus had the motor up front. He put a two or three inch gas pipe from the front all the way to the back, which is about twenty-five feet. You'd come down a hill and let off the gas and it would sound like an attack

15

from Russia coming at you. We'd drive it around Claremore at night, but it made so much noise people complained to the police. We had to park at night unless we were playing out of town. During the day we'd drive to school, I was a senior and would load it up with kids and drive around town. We had a big time with it. I drove it to high school; it was the only transportation I had.

We might be playing Collinsville, Ramona, Pryor, or other towns nearby, and the high school kids would hear about it. They kept up with where we were playing. We would get fifteen to twenty kids on the bus for fifty cents each. That would get them a ride to the dance as well as a ticket to the dance. It gave us gas money and a little to eat on. The band didn't ride on the bus; they drove from Tulsa or from wherever they lived; only Bill and I were the band members on the bus.

The Flex was the premier of buses; Flexible was the name of the company that made them. Bob, Johnnie Lee, Leon, Hank Thompson, they all had one – they were the custom bus back in those days. It only had seats, but we heard about polka bands up north having sleeper busses – however, they were big busses like Greyhound. They had bunks in them. They were the big bands, but western bands didn't put bunks in them. I think Nashville started that. The Flex would hold thirty people. That was the only vehicle I had until I played for Johnnie Lee in '52.

I met Bob Wills in Claremore on Will Rogers Day, November 4th, 1949. They had a big parade, and he had just gotten a new bus from an oil company, boy, it was pretty – maroon and white; and I had that old blue gray thing of mine. He was in the parade, and I was right behind him. I had a lot of guts, but no sense. We were in the parade with him. That night they were playing at the Armory, so we drove that old bus down. Bob was parked near the big double doors on the south side of

16

the Armory. I pulled up right beside him; I was proud as a peacock then. So the steel player and I go over and look at him, sittin' on the bus. Lucky Moeller was sittin' on the bus – he was the owner of the Trianon Ballroom, in Oklahoma City at the time. I asked, "Can we look at your bus"? Bob said, "Sure". Lucky said, "We just got this bus last week". I said, "How much does a bus like this cost"? He said, "Sixteen thousand and five hundred dollars". I thought, "There's not that much money in Oklahoma". I didn't want to tell him we had paid $500 for that piece of junk sittin' there beside it. He took us all through the bus, but Bob didn't come back with us. Lucky was real nice to us young kids. I told him that we had a band, and I said to myself that someday I was going to work with Bob Wills – and I did.

I don't remember when Paul McGhee and I hooked up together, but he had started playing drums with Bill Roy and stayed with us. We had another guitar player named Bill Markel who played just like Junior Bernard, one of the all time great western swing guitarists; he had every lick that Junior played. I played the guitar, but we learned that if I played the bass on the bass strings of the guitar, we had a little four string rhythm swing section. That was Paul's idea.

I was trying to develop my own style in those days, and was influenced by T-Bone Walker. Ernie Fields, the great Tulsa black band leader, had a club down on Greenwood, so Paul and I would slip down to the back of the club and watch through the opening that held a large fan. I heard T-Bone Walker one night; he was from the East Texas area and started recording when he was a teenager. He did all sorts of movements while he played his rhythm and blues; he was a great entertainer. He pushed his strings – his blues licks were pulling and pushing his strings. Junior Bernard got most of his licks from T-Bone, and I sure liked what he played. Even though Tulsa and Oklahoma were segregated at that time, Ernie Fields occasionally would let Paul sit way at the back of the stage and play drums.

One night in Vinita at the 66 Club a big fight broke out. I heard a drastic change on the cymbal – from a real nice cymbal sound to a real ring. I looked around, and Paul had pulled out a long frog sticker (knife) and was playing the cymbal with the blade and motioning to those who were fighting to come on up. In those days you almost had to kick people off the bandstand. I had a man break my fiddle at the Hay Loft in Inola one night. Willard wasn't there to play the fiddle, so when it came time to play a Paul Jones, I played it. That man came up and grabbed the fiddle out of my hand and smashed it. I guess he didn't like the key I was playing the breakdown in. Roy Clugston was a big old tough guy playing the bass; he popped the man pretty hard for breaking it.

Chapter 2
ART DAVIS and JOHNNIE LEE WILLS DAYS

*A*rt Davis grew up in Dallas, Texas and was a swing fiddler starting
in his high school days. He had been an original member of
Roy Newman's band as well as the Bill Boyd and the Cowboy Ramblers
band; in 1935 Gene Autry hired him and took him to Hollywood. There he
appeared in Autry movies and in other B-grade westerns with Bill Boyd
and Ken Maynard. In 1942, during the World War II years, he served in
the U. S. Navy; unfortunately after the war when he returned to Hollywood
and organized The Rhythm Riders, he found limited work with his band.
He moved to Tulsa, where he and his brother Jay, performing as the Davis
Brothers, had a show over KTUL Radio. Then he went to Miami, Oklahoma
where Tommy and the others joined him.

I graduated in May, 1949, and then Paul McGhee, Billy Marple, and
I had a little trio – the Range Riders no longer worked as a band. We
played different places around Vinita, but mainly at "Club 66". Then in
late 1949 Art Davis hired us; he was a good fiddle player and a good band
leader. We went up to Miami, Oklahoma where he had a daily radio show
that we worked; we played a lot of dances in the area and played movie
theaters when movie stars came to the area towns to promote their movie.
The audience could see a movie star and hear a live band led by a former
movie star. Bob Wommack, the great western swing trumpet player, was
there when we joined Art. Art had a pretty big band.

He had a big old Cadillac that had jump seats; you could put five people in the back seat, two up front, and with the driver you had an eight piece band. He also had a trailer. We'd go play, and he would say, "Well, boys, we made about five dollars a piece tonight". He'd give each of us five dollars. The next night we'd go play to maybe 75 people, and he would say, "Well, boys, we didn't do very well tonight, we made about five dollars apiece". The next night we might have four hundred people, he'd say, "Well, boys, we did better tonight, but I had a lot of expenses – posters and all, we cleared about five dollars apiece". We never could get over five dollars apiece.

That spring we went to Hobbs, New Mexico with Art to the La Miradora Club. He said, "I got $35 a week for everybody, but here's the deal – we've got one double room". There were six of us. He had it figured out, and said, "The first four that come to the room at night get the beds, the other two will sleep on the floor. That's why we married so young; we weren't making enough to rent another room". We were all nineteen years old and didn't care. There were six of us kids, Art and an older guy who was a drummer. Art had a trailer house so he stayed in a motor park. Paul McGhee who was our regular drummer wouldn't go to Hobbs; he'd been out there the year before and knew the story, so we took this other guy on drums. He said that if he took a big band out there that a lot of men don't like New Mexico, and three or four men would quit.

When we got ready to leave Miami he had one car, his mobile home and a band trailer. He said that we sure need a man in the band with a car. He got a copy of *Billboard* and there was an ad that said, "Steel guitar player, have nice automobile, will travel – Springfield, Missouri". So Art called this guy; we were playing at Commerce, Oklahoma where Mickey Mantle was from. We were playing a Saturday night dance, and Art told that guy to come down that night, "We're leaving for Hobbs tomorrow".

20

He shows up and has a nice new four door Dodge and had a trailer hitch on it. Art said, "You do have a trailer hitch don't you"? He said, "Oh, yeh, I've been pulling a band trailer". We said, "Are you going' ta play with us tonight"? He said, "No, I think I'll wait 'til we get out ta Hobbs". He looked kind of tired, so that night after we got off we took out for Hobbs. This guy had a load of musicians and was pulling the band trailer; Art, pulling his trailer, had his wife and little girl and a load of musicians.

We get out there, and the very first night we're going to play Art played the theme song which was the "Lone Star Rag"; he goes right into "Milk Cow Blues", and looks at the steel player. This man had a real fine double neck steel, a Fender amp, a towel over his right leg to keep his hands dry – he was all set to go. Art sang a couple of verses and looked at him to take a solo, and he shook his head. Bob Wommack eased over to me and said, "I think we've got problems on the steel". I said, "If he can't play a solo on 'Milk Cow Blues,' I know we've got problems". It turned out that he couldn't play anything; he just made noises that came out of it. He said, "I forgot to tell you that I was just learning". Art paid him for a week and sent him back home.

We weren't in Hobbs long when Art said, "Tommy, I want you to go with me; I've got my brother Jay – he's gonna come in – along with some of the boys". Now this is after we had been there about a week. We started traveling with the mayor of Roswell who was running for governor of New Mexico; his name was Lake Frazier. While we were traveling with the mayor we started talking about that steel guy, and Art said, "Well, you know I bring all those fellows out there; most of them were goin' ta quit after a few weeks and our band was goin' ta be back down to regular size and then I can give everybody a raise – you know, we'll do alright". He had sent the steel player home; then Buddy Kendricks got homesick. We

21

had a little seventeen year old Italian boy from Columbus, Kansas who got homesick for his "momma".

We were out the first week on the campaign with Bob Wommack on trumpet, Jay Davis on piano, Coony Conrad the drummer, Art and me – a five piece band. He then called Caesar Massey to come in and play fiddle for a couple of weeks while we were out touring with this guy. Art was getting big bucks touring with this mayor running for governor. I later told Bob that the club job was just to get us out there so he could tour with Lake Frazier. Art was a good man, a good band leader, but he was on a down hill run at that time in his life and career. He had had a big band for years and at one time did well.

When we would actually be working in Hobbs, we would get Sunday nights off. Two or three of us would go over and sit in and jam with a black band – Sunshine Butler's Orchestra. Sunshine Butler was a great big band and old time Dixieland drummer. He always had excellent black musicians coming through, either going to or coming from California. One of them was the great Chubby Krank, a be-bop trumpeter. They could play a blues number for thirty minutes. In those days, New Mexico would shut down on Sundays, so on three different occasions we went to Big Springs, Texas to play dances with them. I got paid for working with them – $10 a dance and all you could drink. Art got wind about what we were doing, and he sarcastically said, "I don't care if you go over there; you're as good as they are". For me, it was a great learning experience.

I'd get high riding with them – they all smoked pot and I had to breathe. I'd sit there like a statue, and they thought it was funny because I couldn't talk. Pot was new to me; I'd never been around it. I was a teenager scared to death, and I can guarantee that you get the effects of pot in a car with all the windows rolled up.

Tommy's band at the Shamrock Club, Lawton, Oklahoma, 1951; l to r: Tommy Allsup, leader and guitar; Bob White, steel guitar; Glenn "Blub" Reese, saxophone; Dutch Ingram, drums; Bob Wommack, trumpet; Donnie McDaniels, piano. "Bob Wommack was the greatest western swing trumpet man ever".

Bob and I split from Art, and went to work for a kid in Carlsbad, New Mexico, Jim Ed Stewart, who had a big western swing band and played Bob Wills music. That's what we liked, and he was from Lawton, Oklahoma. When his contract in Carlsbad was up that fall – September 1950 – we went to Lawton, but he was drafted into military service almost as soon as we got there. It was the Korean War period. So I took over the band; that's how I got to Lawton.

That same month, September 1950, Paul McGhee and I were hired to play two nights in Big Springs, Texas at the Yales Inn. We were setting up that afternoon when Lefty Frizzell came by and said that he was looking for a band to go on the road and go to Dallas to make records for Columbia. He told us, "I'm gonna be a star, but my band don't want

23

to travel with me". He wasn't well known at that time, and we were suspicious about a man whose band didn't want to travel with him. He was going to record some of this early songs that helped make him a super star, and we ate crow two years later when we heard him on the radio.

After Lefty's third hit came out, he came to Lawton to play the Southern Club; we were working the Shamrock Club, and after our last set, "Blub" Reese, Bob Wommack, and I went to hear him. We pulled in behind the Southern Club and heard that Lefty had whipped his band. He had been a boxer and could really fight. Someone in the band said something that pissed him off. The club owner thought it was funny and told us, "Lefty whipped four guys in the band up there on the stage". They were wearing white shirts and had bloody noses. Lefty had on a new uniform and not a scratch on it; the owner said that he was like a tiger when he went after them. We changed our opinion about him and liked him a little better but were glad we weren't in his band. He was a stylist; you knew who he was when he sang.

When we first got to Lawton we played the Shamrock Club and later the Southern Club – we played eighteen months in 1950 and all of 1951 without a day off. The band was Bob Wommack, trumpet; Bob White, steel guitar; Glenn "Blub" Reese, saxophone; Donny McDaniels, piano; Dutch Ingram, drums; and me on the guitar. Bob Wommack was the best western swing trumpet player ever, and we had a good band.

Then in early 1952 a fiddle player from Tulsa named Johnny Leach came down and said, "I've got a deal in Tulsa on a radio station". I said, "Let's go". We had played nearly a year and a half without a night off; the whole band was ready to go. So we returned to Tulsa where KRMG Radio was just getting started. So we played a radio show with Johnny Leach.

Bill Roy and Tommy Allsup.

At that time, the radio stations didn't pay a band to play; instead, the band played free to advertise dances. Johnny had only enough money to keep the band together for about six weeks before it blew up. Then Bill Roy and I went to Wichita, Kansas, to work with Jimmy Hall who was an excellent vocalist and fiddle player. He had been with Leon McAuliffe for a few years, but had left Leon and had a band at the Cowboy Inn. Unfortunately, not long after we got there the Cowboy Inn was caught serving liquor to minors; the State took their liquor license away sometime in the fall of 1952. I was out of a job.

Bill Wimberly had a band and a radio show in Wichita, and he also was traveling over and playing the Red Foley shows in Springfield on the weekends. Gene Crownover was playing the steel guitar with him at that time. Wimberly said, "Tommy, Johnnie Lee Wills is looking for a guitar player; do you want to go to Tulsa"? I said, "Do I? *Take me back to Tulsa*"! I was ready! He called Johnnie Lee, and I moved to Tulsa in the fall of 1952 , maybe October, and stayed until late summer 1953.

Johnnie Lee Wills was one of the original Texas Playboys who came to Tulsa with his brother Bob on February 9, 1934. As a Playboy he played the tenor banjo as a rhythm instrument, but he played the guitar as a backup instrument for their father while they lived in west Texas – and he was a swing fiddler in his own band. In 1938 Bob kept telling him to move his chair back further on the stage. He recalled that when he told Bob that if he moved back any more he would be off of the stage, Bob smiled and made him organize his own band. Johnnie Lee's first band was not successful; his second band in 1940 had some of the Playboys and a few former Alabama Boys, which was a band that brought many excellent swing musicians to Tulsa. This Johnnie Lee band sparked, and when Bob left Tulsa, he made Johnnie Lee take Cain's, the annual rodeo and the KVOO Radio shows. In many communities and regions Johnnie Lee Wills and All His Boys became more popular than Bob and the Playboys. As with Bob, Johnnie Lee was not the best swing fiddler, but he was an excellent band leader and in the early '50s had the best western swing band in the nation.

I never will forget Johnnie Lee. At that time Leon McAuliffe, who also headquartered in Tulsa, had Bouncin' Bobby Bruce and Jimmy Hall – those guys would jump three feet and run all over the bandstand when they took a solo. Johnnie Lee said, "Tommy, I'd like for you to work with us, but we're not like Leon's band. We don't jump around; we're more of a

Advertisement for the Johnnie Lee Wills show over KVOO Radio, Tulsa, when Tommy was in the band, 1953.

solemn type band. I just want you to play good; you don't have to jump up every time you play a solo". I took Don Tolle's place on the band. Tommy Elliot was playing steel. We had a good group, and Johnnie Lee still had horns. He had Cotton Thompson, Curly Lewis, Henry Boatman on fiddles, his brother Luke on bass, Wade Peeler on drums, Clarence Cagle on the piano and Fred Beatty on sax. Don Harland had left, but he came back for awhile. Luke stood between me and Clarence Cagle when we played.

We had Fender amps, took the cloth off and put on zebra cloth. It was a fabric that looked like a zebra skin; it was Tommy Elliott the steel player's idea. I still had mine when we went back to Lawton. Then we bought uniforms and sent pictures to the Pan-American Livestock Show in Houston, Texas; they hired us to play the Show in January 1953.

At that time Johnnie Lee had a better band than Bob. Johnnie Lee had men who had worked with him for years and of course he wasn't traveling much. But Bob was working California, the West Coast, Texas, Oklahoma – he was traveling all the time. You couldn't have a home and travel; Johnnie Lee's men could and did make their home in Tulsa. When I was with Johnnie Lee, Bob was working out of Amarillo, then Dallas, then Fort Worth – Bob worked Texas solid and had a big following in south Texas.

The furthest we drove to play a dance when I was with Johnnie Lee was Laredo, Texas. This was a Texas tour when we played the Pan-American Livestock Show. In Laredo we were supposed to go to a place that had a world famous New Orleans gin fizz. Luke was telling me this; he told me that this was the greatest drink there ever was. So Luke, Tommy Elliott, Wade Peeler and myself hired one of these little buggies and went back across the border in Nuevo Laredo to this little place that had signs that said, "World Famous Gin Fizz". It was good; I never had another one like it, but our dinner was not what it should have been. I ordered a roast duck dinner, and I think I got a mud hen. Luke said that he thought it was crow, but what the hell, the gin fizzes made it a trip worth while. The buggy ride only cost a dollar. It was a lot of fun, but that was as far from Tulsa that we traveled when I was in the band.

We had big crowds, and when we were gone KVOO played those 16" transcriptions. The interesting thing is that one time while we were gone Hank Williams played at Cain's; it was late December 1952 when we got back in time for the New Year's Eve dance. Hank was there about a week earlier, and he died on New Year's Day in 1953. Mr. Mayo told us that Hank and his doctor driver came in the office before he went on the bandstand to perform – his band was already playing – and said that he would like to have a beer. They weren't supposed to but they had a little bar that sold beer, so they got him a beer. Mr. Mayo said that he drank about a third of that beer and was high; I always wondered how that could happen. I guess his resistance was so low. He went on the stage and put on a whale of a show, got off the stage, went out the back door, got in the back seat of his car and passed out. Mr. Mayo said that he could hardly walk to the bandstand, but when he put that guitar strap around his neck he started singing. To me that was an incredible story. I was twenty-one years old, and a story like that upset me a little. At that time we didn't know about the drugs; that doctor was driving him and keeping him hopped up on something.

We would start out each week with the Monday broadcast, and then head out maybe 200 miles to play a dance. Thursday was all gospel music, and when he did gospel he would leave out the horns and the drums. Usually it was two fiddles, guitar, steel, piano and bass. Friday we would be back on the road, and Saturday we were back home at Cain's. There was always a big crowd that showed up for the noon broadcast. I would always bring my dad and mother over for it. My dad and Johnnie Lee became pretty good friends. Dad was an old time fiddler who remembered when the Playboys started broadcasting over KVOO. The trio was Curly, Henry and Tommy Elliott (*steel player*) while I was in it; Don Harland left the band while I was there.

We had a Thursday night broadcast that wasn't more than an hour or two long; the Saturday night broadcast was from midnight til 1:00; we received letters from all over the western states. Johnnie Lee said that he even got one from Hawaii. When we were traveling down the road, if we passed a vegetable stand, Johnnie Lee would always stop and get some onions. He liked onions; he'd make a sandwich with a slice of baloney and onions and would eat an onion like an apple.

I never did see Johnnie Lee drunk. I wasn't around him that much, but I went to many of his dances before I ever played with him. I used to come over to Cain's when I was sixteen years old. I saw Spade Cooley, Luke's band, Tommy Duncan's band – they had some good drinkers in those bands. Bob Wommack was pretty good at it; we had a lot of practice up at Miami with Art Davis. When Bob went to Korea he told me he did everything he could to get out of the army. He told them that he wet the bed at night, because he had heard that bed wetting would get you discharged. He said that every night they would wake him at two o'clock and four o'clock and make him go to the latrine. After five nights of this he told them that he wasn't a bed wetter. Shortly before he died, I used him on the Billy Mize tribute to Tommy Duncan; he was a great Duncan fan.

Our bus was that old Flex that Johnnie Lee had with no bunks, just seats. We'd be coming in late at night, trying to sleep and Tilly Roach, the driver had a voice as loud as Clarence Cagle's. When Clarence talked you could hear him; he had a good booming voice. I never could figure it out – why didn't he sit behind Tilly so they could talk? Clarence would sit at least half way back, so if you were sitting between Clarence and Tilly, you weren't going to get much sleep. I guess Clarence wanted to keep Tilly awake, but it sounded like a couple of lions roaring.

You stepped down in the well to urinate; in other words, you stepped down to the door and the driver cracked the door enough to let you relieve yourself. It probably was dangerous because after those dances not all of the men were sober. There probably was rust down the door side of the bus. I heard that Johnny Duncan was with Johnnie Lee for a week or two but left when they wouldn't stop the bus; he thought that they were crazy for stepping down in the well.

We had plenty of experience at drinking. I was pretty young. One night we played McAlester, and Wade got drunk and just puked all over

30

his snare drum. So Johnnie Lee said, "We'll just cut out the drinking; no more drinking in the band". Poor old Cotton had to have a drink, he had done it so long that he had to. He was out of the old school with Mancel Tierney and those guys. In fact, one night we were playing – Luke was standing by me and Cotton stood right in front of the drums. Johnnie Lee, Curly, and Henry were the front line playing. Cotton never would stand up on the front line with the fiddles. He didn't play in the section; he would jump in and play solos and sing but didn't play in the fiddle section. Luke had gone out to get a Coke, and someone had filled it with whiskey. Somebody had brought Luke some whiskey. They called Cotton "Whitey;" he kept looking around. Luke said, "What're you lookin' at Whitey"? Cotton said, while he was lickin' his lips 'cause he just knew something was in that Coke, "What do you have there"? Luke said, "It's just a Coke; Johnnie Lee said no more drinking on the bandstand". Johnnie Lee had eyes in the back of his head and could see Cotton looking at that drink. After about ten minutes, Cotton couldn't stand it any longer and went over and poured it all down. Johnnie Lee turned around, and Cotton spit all that he had in his mouth all over Luke and said, "Damn it, Luke, why didn't you tell me you had whiskey in that damn drink"!

I don't remember anyone getting so drunk that they couldn't play. I never did see Johnnie Lee drink much; in fact, only Wade and Cotton drank very much. There really wasn't that much drinking going on in Johnnie Lee's band. When Wade threw up on his snare drum, Johnnie Lee cut it all off. I disagree with those who say that Johnnie Lee was a heavy drinker.

In 1951/52 General Mills for their products Larro Feed and Red Star Flour was geared to promote Johnnie Lee Wills and His Boys as

"America's Finest Western Recording Band". In Tulsa, the broadcast time was 12:30 p. m., Monday thru Saturday over KVOO Radio. In other radio markets the broadcast time varied and different General Mills products sponsored the show. There was the "Johnnie Lee Wills Radio Special / Buy a Sack Today! / PurAsnow Enriched Flour", 10:15 a. m., Monday, Wednesday, and Friday radio shows. They cut many transcriptions (16" discs), but the shows just didn't go over in the markets out of the Southwest. General Mills dropped him. The rumor was that the reason it didn't really develop was that Johnnie Lee drank too much. That was just before I went on the band and they had finished the transcriptions, but I had never heard the drinking rumors. My opinion is that those people came up here and heard Johnnie Lee's band with the horns and drums, and when they cut them, they used the same band as the Gospel show – no horns or drums. It was not the Johnnie Lee Wills sound. It was the completely different sound from what they bought for the project. They used too many public domain songs; using Stephen Foster songs was not the Johnnie Lee Wills style. And they didn't want to pay the complete band; it was an economy project that killed the Johnnie Lee Wills sound. That's the problem with the upper level of those companies; they approve a project and immediately look at the bottom line, and cut the costs that make the project original and unique which kills the original project. I never could figure out why the top men could and would kill quality.

"Milk Cow Blues" was Cotton's number, but the 1941 Decca record was nothing compared to how he was singing it ten years later. Cotton died in '53. He was singing "There's Good Rockin' Tonight" back in those days – he was rockin' and rollin' on Johnnie Lee's band. The horns had those riffs behind him – it was better than the Bill Haley stuff. He was doing rocking blues – he was doin' "Georgia on My Mind". Cotton had that rockabilly feel to his music. He was doin' it way before Elvis and those guys.

I cut a transcription with Johnnie Lee; it was "Three Little Blue Birds on a Window Sill", or something like that – came out on Bullet. I have said that my first recording was with Wade Ray in 1956, but I guess it was with Johnnie Lee.

We were playing Cain's one night, and this couple was dancing right in front of the stage and her drawers fell. Evidently the safety pin broke, and they were hanging around her ankles. I thought that she would trip. She never missed a step, and stepped right out of them and kicked them up on the stage. They came right over Johnnie Lee's and Curly's head – you can ask Curly Lewis – and hit Wade Peeler, the drummer, right in the face. Wade was trying to knock them off with a stick; he finally got those big old drawers on the end of his stick and was slinging them around in a circle and they came loose and hit Luke right in the face. He swiped them off and threw them down by the steel guitar player. Johnnie Lee was beside himself – embarrassed. But we were all so tickled that the old gal never missed a step – it was as if it were staged. The elastic had probably broken, and she had them pinned up. And they weren't dainty little bikinis; they were big old drawers – a pair that two people could have gotten into.

I liked Johnnie Lee; he was a solid person. I stayed with him for nearly a year. I was there when Uncle John died, and Bob came back and stayed around for awhile. Everybody did their own job, but I had reached a point in my life when I wanted my own band. I liked what he was playing, but I had had a good band when I was in Lawton. We played Lawton one night, and a man came around to me and said, "I sure do wish you'd come back and take over this band". They made me an offer I couldn't refuse. I guess I quit because I wanted to run my own band again. Except for a short time in California in 1955, I was in Lawton until 1959.

The first time I got married was in Lawton playing at the Southern Club; Bobby White, Paul McGhee, and I all had girl friends and got a whim to get married. We went to Wichita Falls and were married. My wife's name was Joy Newport; she was a year older than I. We were divorced in 1955. My daughter from that marriage is Gayla; she lives in Nashville. My marriage lasted about two and a half years.

After the divorce, I decided to go to California; my brother Kenneth lived out there, and I figured that I could find work in the Los Angeles area. I started working days in a General Motors car assembly plant and at night looked for places to play, so I went to a place called the Hitching Post Club where Herb Tucker worked. They needed a guitar player and asked me to sit in. I did, and he said, "My brother needs a guitar player; you want to work"? I said, "Yeh, but I can't get in the union because of the waiting period". He introduced me to his brother, Jack Tucker, a country singer from Ada, Oklahoma.

Jack had a group called the Oklahoma Playboys, and they worked on Friday and Saturday nights at Foreman Phillips' County Barn Dance in Baldwin Park. Jack was a good country singer, but played bad rhythm guitar. He had a Fender Telecaster that was hard to keep in tune, but he had a big following in California. He decided to hire me, but I didn't have the union card. Jack took me to the Union Hall and said, "I'm going to hire him because he plays western swing guitar and sings songs". There weren't many western swing guitarists in California at that time. They gave me a card, but if any guitarist who had been in the union longer than I wanted the job, I was to be bumped.

Working at the County Barn Dance was fun. People ask about

Foreman Phillips, but he had died before I got there. I didn't know him. However, he had been a disc jockey in Southern California when he promoted his first County Barn Dances at Venice Pier in 1942; there he promoted both Spade Cooley and Bob Wills – he had over fifteen thousand show up for one Wills dance. Then he moved to Baldwin Park where they had a big dance hall. Phillips promoted Spade Cooley and many believe that with Cooley, he popularized the term "western swing". But I've been told that during one of Bob's recording sessions, Art Satherly said, "Bob, the band is really swinging; I think we ought to call it western swing". Spade Cooley was the Lawrence Welk of western swing; he only used arrangements, and western swing is at its best when you play it off the top of your head. I think western swing really started to jell around 1945.

My first real recording session was with Wade Ray while I was in California – February 1956. At that time he was an RCA Victor artist, so Chet Atkins and Steve Scholes came out to Los Angeles to record him. Wade was a great western swing fiddler and singer. I had been out there a few months playing in the Jack Tucker Oklahoma Playboys band – making good money, but the music wasn't too good. It wasn't the music I wanted to play. Wade was right down the street in Cow Town, and had a good band. Jimmy Wyble was his guitarist but had been hired away by the Red Norvo Trio, so Wade gave me the job. I had worked with him back in Oklahoma when he was there in a battle of the bands session.

We recorded a Jimmie Rodgers song: "Any Old Time You Want to Come Back Home". I remember that session because Chet Atkins said, "Do you have a flat top guitar, and can you play some open chords"? I said, "No, I don't have a flat top guitar, and I don't know any open chords – what are you talking about"? He said the arrangement was in B flat,

The Tommy Allsup Band, l to r Dale Burkett, piano; Freddie Franks, fiddle; Dale Wilson, fiddle; Clint Badgwell, drums; Tommy Allsup, leader and guitar; Roy Wilcox, bass; Bill Roy, steel.

Tommy shaking hands with Red Foley at the Southern Club, Lawton, Oklahoma, 1953.

The Southern Club band, Lawton, Oklahoma, 1953; l to r, back row: Bob, piano; Tommy Allsup; Mike, trumpet;front row: Nat, fiddle; Bennie Wallace, drums; Richard Dozier, bass; Bill Roy.

and that if I put a capo on I could play an open A. Wade said that he thought I didn't understand what Chet was saying; he was right. Chet was trying to tell me how the rhythm guitar was played in Nashville. *They were playing what Oreon Yates and Art Davis had beat me in the head not to play!* He said, "Can you turn all the treble up on that Fender and let your chords ring out"? I had no earthly

Bob Wills, Tommy Allsup, Johnnie Lee Wills

"This photo with Bob Wills and Johnnie Lee Wills was made at the Southern Club; Johnnie Lee and Bob were working together at that time. It was 1958: I left the Southern Club and didn't go back after 1958".

idea of what he was talking about. Wade said, "I think we'll just let him play like he plays in my band". I've always thanked Wade for that; when I got to Nashville in 1963 with Willie Nelson, I knew what they were talking about – they were all playing those open chords and letting them ring out.

When Chet suggested a capo, I didn't even know what he was talking about. When I was a boy, we used to take a pencil and put it on a string, wrap it around the neck, and clamp it down; the nut was so high that this got the strings down on the frets where you could play. But I had no idea what a capo was. I got trapped in those Nashville sessions and now own a flat top guitar and a capo, but I can play in B flat and "let those strings ring out". The average person doesn't know if I have a capo on or not. But a capo is as important as a pick to some guitar players.

You know, when I was playing with Jack Tucker's little country band, we were doing a radio show one night at Harmony Park Ballroom along with the Maddox Brothers and Rose. Fred Maddox of the Maddox Brothers was playing the bass and would slap that old bass in the open strings – G, D, A, and E. Biff Collie was the announcer at KFOX Radio; Biff came up and was going to do a song like "Bill Bailey". Fred yelled, "What key is it in"? Biff replied, "It's in B flat". Fred said, "Where's that"? I held up two fingers about two inches, and said, "About that far from A". He said, "If it ain't no further than that, why don't you just play it in A"! He always slapped those upper strings. They were a great entertaining family band, but it didn't make much difference what key you were in, the bass was rarely there.

When I was in Johnnie Lee Wills' band, Luke Wills used to say, "Tommy, I've got thirteen licks on the bass". We'd be playing and I would hear a little run and look back at him; he would hold up four fingers, and a few numbers later I would hear a run and he would hold up seven fingers. He had each run numbered; he was a funny man, and had the best sense of humor among the four Wills brothers.

I had met Louise Rowe, and we were married in late 1955. Louise was a good musician and singer; in fact, she probably was the first female to be a musician, not just a singer, for Bob Wills and the Texas Playboys. She played bass for Bob about the same time that I worked for Johnnie Lee. Prior to that Louise had worked with her brothers in the Seven Rowe Brothers band. It was in March 1956 when they called for me and Louise to come back to the Southern Club in Lawton. I figured that we would be there for a long time, but in the winter of '57, the Southern Club was shut down for bootlegging. So we moved out to Snuffy Smith's Club in Hobbs, New Mexico, for three months – December, January, and February – then back to Lawton. Later in 1958, Louise and I were divorced.

When I was in Lawton I did a lot of touring with Tommy Duncan. Sam Gibbs would book tours in Texas, and I would take my band to back Tommy. Tommy Duncan didn't drink; Bob Wommack was in my band, and Bob could drink. We started playing in bands together, and I don't know how he got so good at drinking and I didn't. But Tommy liked Bob, and Bob worshiped Tommy. So one day Tommy said, "Why don't you let Bob ride with me"? He did and from that day on when we toured with Tommy, Bob wouldn't take a drink – he wouldn't take a drink in front Duncan. We would come back to the Southern Club, and Bob would fall off the wagon and the stage.

We were playing one night in Lawton and a man came up to Tommy. Now, Sid, the man who owned the Southern Club was the toughest man on earth – nice, friendly; he could take a three hundred pound block of ice and run up two flights of stairs. He loved Tommy Duncan about as much as Bob Wommack did. This man came up to Tommy and said, "Do you remember when we got drunk"? Tommy said, "You didn't get drunk with me, because I don't drink". The man said, "Why you son of a bitch, are you saying you didn't get drunk with me"? And he pulled out a big long knife and started to take a swing at Tommy. Sid always stood at the side of the bandstand when Tommy sang. He took that man's hand and crushed it. No matter what people might say, I don't believe that Tommy ever took a drink.

The older musicians who drank were different. I remember that Jesse Ashlock told me when they were with us in Lawton, that Louie Tierney would say, "Loan me a little so I can get a pint". Jesse would say, "I don't have any money", and would open his billfold to show that he didn't. I asked him where he hid his money, and he said, "In Louie's billfold; he never looks there".

39

Leon McAuliffe didn't drink. When he left the Playboys to go into the military in 1942, he didn't see Bob again until 1956. We had the night off at the Southern Club, so I went to Wichita Falls – Keith Coleman and Cecil Brower were playing in Leon's band and so was Billy Dozier – we were going to have a jam session at the Southern Club. Bob's band was playing there, and he had Billy Bowman on steel. I picked up Keith, Cecil, and Leon in my car and took them to Lawton. We got to the Club and they said that Bob was over in the motel with Luke. In Wichita Falls you played until midnight, but at the Southern Club we played until 2 p. m. So Bob's group was still playing.

There was a little motel where the bands stayed that was across the creek from the club. We walked over to the motel, knocked on the door, and went in. Bob was sitting there growling like an old bear – he had not seen Leon since 1942. Leon had his red Nudie suit that had rhinestone panhandles on it standing for his "Panhandle Rag". The first words that Bob uttered after all those years were, "Son, I thought I taught you better than to wear shit that looks like that". Leon's mouth dropped open, and he said, "Well, Bob I had this suit made for my 'Panhandle Rag' song". Bob said, "Oh, I know it". He got up and hugged Leon's neck.

Leon told him that we were going to have a jam session at the Southern Club, and Bob replied, "We're playing over there". I think he was drinking a little. He said, "I've already quit for the night, but if you're going to play, I'll come over". We went over and went in the back door; the Club was closed. They had black waiters at the Club, and they were cleaning up. Bob thought the dance was still going on and stepped up to the microphone and said, "Folks, I want you to meet the first steel guitar player in my band – the best ever, and now he's going to play 'The Steel Guitar Rag'". Leon didn't know what to do. Billy Bowman's steel was still set up, but he sat down to play and Leon always stood up and – Leon played a four necked steel. So Leon sits down, and his knees are taller than Bowman's guitar was. Leon sat there with that guitar between his legs and played "Steel Guitar Rag".

Cecil Brower had really been hitting the bottle, and Bob still thought the dance was going on. He introduced Cecil as one he worked with as a Lightcrust Doughboy. Cecil can just barely stand up. Keith Coleman and I used to laugh about this for years. Cecil would walk to the mike to play and then start falling backward; Luke would grab him and hold him up to the mike. Bob kept introducing people – he introduced Ted Adams who had come up from Wichita and had his bass ready.

We had a dressing room at the side of the stage. The stage was a two tier outfit with a small piano sitting on the second tier. The bass stood back there by the piano and the drums were in the middle. Ted said, "Get your guitar". So I set my amp back by Teddy; I had my leg over that little piano. Bob would look back and stare at me. Keith came back and said, "Bob's wondering what his guitar player's doing". The chair for the guitar player was empty. It was like the time they put the mannequin where the bass player stood and hung the electric bass around it, and Bob said to Eldon Shamblin, "We got to fire that bass player – he's no good". Keith said that Bob was worried about his guitarist sitting on the piano, but he never said anything to me about coming up and sitting where I belonged. Keith was dying laughing, because about every four minutes Bob would turn around and stare with those dark eyes of his. Leon was still over there trying to play the steel which looked like a toy between his legs. This went on for about forty-five minutes; then Bob told everybody goodnight. Luke and Sam Gibbs took him back to the motel, and he went to bed. But he always thought he was playing the dance.

The Southern Club in Lawton was sort of home base for me between working with Johnnie Lee, Bob, and Buddy – all the years I worked around them. But I left the Southern Club and didn't go back after 1958. When Buddy Holly got killed I had just left Lawton. We would book other clubs for six weeks at a time; in the winter of '57, I had Louie and Mancel Tierney with me down in Lawton and we booked Snuffy Smith's Club in Hobbs, New Mexico. In December, 1958 we were in Odessa, Texas, playing at a club that had once been a strip joint and had been converted into a western club called the Silver Saddle. That's when I went on tour with Buddy, because my booking was up just before that tour started.

Chapter 3
CLOVIS and BUDDY HOLLY

O n September 7, 1936 Charles Hardin Holley was born at 1911
6th Street in Lubbock, Texas, the youngest of four children born
to Lawrence and Ella Holley; he soon became known as Buddy Holly
(he dropped the "e" for stage purposes). It was a traditional musical
family with country and gospel music played at family gatherings and for
relaxation. Buddy decided that music would be his career and as a teenager
began recording western and bop demonstration records. He signed with
Decca Records in January, 1956 and did a Sonny James tour and a Hank
Thompson tour; Sonny Curtis and Don Guess worked with him as the
Two Tones and later Jerry Allison joined them and they became the Three
Tunes. The Decca tunes recorded in Nashville did not get promoted. In
January, 1957 again they toured with Hank Thompson, a tour that included
Wanda Jackson, Cowboy Copas, George Jones, and other country stars.
In February, 1957 he formed a backup group with Jerry Allison (drums),
Niki Sullivan (rhythm guitar), and Joe B. Mauldin (bass) to record at the
Norman Petty Studio in Clovis, New Mexico. By August, 1957 they were
recording and appearing as Buddy Holly and The Crickets; they played
shows in Washington, D. C. and Baltimore, Maryland before making their
legendary appearances at the Apollo Theater in New York. Those shows
were followed by a three month tour, September thru November, billed as
"The Biggest Show of Stars for 1957"; most of the acts such as Chuck Berry
and Laverne Baker were African-American, so in some communities where
segregation laws forbidding blacks and whites to appear on the same stage

Buddy Holly during the Winter Dance Tour, 1959; photo by Larry L. Matti, Green Bay, Wisconsin.

existed, Buddy Holly and The Crickets, Paul Anka, The Everly Brothers and Jimmy Bowen could not work the shows. However, this occurred only in a few towns; the tour traveled from New York to California and from Texas to Canada.

On September 19, 1957 their song "That'll Be the Day" hit the charts as the number one hit and stayed in the charts for sixteen weeks; in November "Peggy Sue" quickly rose to the number three position. Buddy Holly was destined to become a legendary rock and roll performer and musical innovator.

In January 1958, they were an act with The Everly Brothers tour which was followed by appearances in Hawaii and Australia. In late February they did the "Big Gold Record Stars" tour with The Everly Brothers, Jerry Lee Lewis and Bill Haley and His Comets; the British Tour was almost the entire month of March which was followed by Alan Freed's Big Beat Show from late March to mid-May.

44

In April 1958, I was back playing the Southern Club in Lawton when I got this call from Jim Ed Stewart, the Lawton boy with whom I had played with back in 1950. He had earned a master's degree in music and was teaching school in Portales, New Mexico. He had three good singers he wanted to record. Jim Ed called me and said, "I'm going to do a session with these three boys in Norman Petty's Studio in Clovis; can you come out and work"? I said, "Sure". So I grabbed my guitar and amp and headed for Clovis, New Mexico. We recorded their songs in one night. Norman Petty had a good drummer and a good bass man on staff as well as a vocal backup group called The Roses; this group had been formed at the Odessa Junior College a few years earlier and included Robert Linville, Ray Rush and David Bingham. Norman's wife, Vi, played the piano. After the session Petty said, "I need a guitar player, can you stay a few days and do some more sessions?" I said, "Sure". I stayed almost a month before getting back to Lawton.

He had sessions almost every night; he was producing constantly. The next night he had a group called the Bowman Brothers who were on Columbia Records, so I did a session with them. Then he had a group come in from Albuquerque – a rock and roll band without a guitar – so I did a session with them. It was the third or fourth night when Buddy Holly came in. I believe he had just returned from England and worked Alan Freed's Big Beat Show. He came in and I met him; he said, "I like what you were doing in that last session; do you want to record with me later in the week"? I said, "Sure". We recorded two or three nights in a row – did a song called "It's So Easy", and I did a solo on it. Then we cut "Heartbeat", and I did a solo on it. Then we cut "Love's Made A Fool Of You", and I did a solo. Buddy played a rhythm type guitar style, so up to that point he had not had any real guitar solos on his records. I played the first guitar solo on a Buddy Holly recording.

Riverside Ballroom, Green Bay, Wisconsin; the Winter Dance was played there the night before the fatal crash. Photo by Larry L. Matti, Green Bay, Wisconsin.

After the sessions I went back to Lawton, and not long afterward a couple of the records I had cut with him were released – "It's So Easy" and "Heartbeat". Buddy had a tour coming up in July, so they wanted to get those recordings released early to help promote the tour. Buddy liked my guitar solos and wanted me to make the tour with him. He called and asked if I could make it; again, I said, "Sure". It was promoted as the Summer Dance Party, so Buddy said, "Get me some horns, and put together a little blues rock band".

I knew Fred Beatty from the Johnnie Lee Wills days and another good sax player from Oklahoma City named Freddie Bunch. I got those two and they had an Indian friend who was playing trumpet with them. We wound up with a trumpet, alto sax, tenor sax, an upright bass player and a drummer, and a kid named Earl Sinks who sang. I played guitar with the dance band and then with Buddy in his show. The bass player had been in an orchestra that played in Oklahoma City, and they let him go while they were working

46

Summer Dance Party, Summer, 1958: Frank Goff, trumpet; Fred Beatty, saxophone; Freddie Bunch, small saxophone; Danny Lucas, drums; Roy Wilcox, bass; Tommy Allsup, guitar.

The Crickets, the Winter Dance Tour, 1959; l to r: Carl Bunch, drums; Waylon Jennings, electric bass; Tommy Allsup, guitar.

Frankie Sardo, vocalist; Tommy Allsup, guitar.

J. P. "The Big Bopper" Richardson, vocalist; Tommy Allsup, guitar, in the background.

there. We found out why he was fired later; he was a heroin addict. We caught him mainlining in a hotel room; he was weird but a hell of a bass player. Danny Lucas from Hobbs was our drummer; he smoked grass and stayed high a lot of the time.

One night Danny was driving and Freddie Bunch would say, "What river is that"? Danny would say, "Man, I don't know; it's the Missouri, man". Freddie was wanting to see the Mississippi River, and said, "Wake me up when you see it". When we got there Freddie asked, "What river are we crossing"? Danny said, "Man, it's the Old Man River, man"; every other word was "man".

It was a fun tour; we had a good time. Buddy bought a new station wagon for the dance band to travel in, and we were a good band. We played the blues, and those horns had some great riffs worked out. The horn players really got off on it. They had played around Oklahoma City and Tulsa with Johnnie Lee Wills and Merl Lindsay and His Oklahoma Night Riders to older crowds, and we were up there playing to three or four thousand a night with young people screaming and hollering. Those guys really loved it; we were a blues band more than a western swing band. We would play about an hour and then Buddy and The Crickets would come out, and I would work with them.

We were out on the road for about two weeks, and played dances in Indiana, Illinois, Michigan, Iowa, Minnesota, and Wisconsin. It was Buddy Holly and The Crickets and the Tommy Allsup Band, and in some towns local bands were used to kick off or to open the dance. It was fun working with Buddy. You know, Buddy's whole career was only about a year and a half – very short. Alan Freed really used him; in late '57 he did the Biggest Show of Stars tour and the Alan Freed Christmas Holiday of Stars Show. Then in January of '58 he toured with the Everly Brothers show followed by shows in Hawaii and Australia; then in March they did the big tour in England. He was young and was used by Norman Petty, Alan Freed and others; when "Peggy Sue" was real hot they ran him all over the country. Entertainers today could not keep up with what they had Buddy Holly doing, and I was with him during the last third of his career.

When the Summer Dance Tour was over we did some more recordings back in Clovis; that's when Buddy produced his Waylon Jennings session. We brought in King Curtis, the black sax player who had played on "Yackety, Yak" with the Coasters. We brought him in to do those sessions, and then Buddy did a lot of demos on his own new material to send to various people like the Everly Brothers. Those demos came out later on Buddy Holly albums, and instead of going back to Lawton I went to Odessa, Texas and the Silver Saddle Club.

Ritchie Valens, playing drums at the Riverside Ballroom, Green Bay, Wisconsin; Tommy Allsup, guitar; Waylon Jennings, bass with back to the camera; photo by Larry L. Matti, Green Bay, Wisconsin.

Ritchie Valens, back stage, Riverside Ballroom, Green Bay, Wisconsin. Photo by Larry L. Matti, Green Bay, Wisconsin.

Dion and The Belmonts; Waylon Jennings, bass; Tommy Allsup, guitar in center; others unidentified.

L to r:
Waylon Jennings,
Tommy Allsup,
Buddy Holly.

Buddy's next tour was a big package tour in October 3-19, 1958 – one of those General Artists Corporation (GAC) "Biggest Show of Stars for 1958" package tours with twelve or more acts. We played all up and down the East Coast from Montreal, Canada to Norfolk, Virginia. Buddy had married Maria Elena Santiago on August 15, 1958 just before that tour and had moved to New York. The tour included Buddy Holly and The Crickets, Frankie Avalon, Bobby Darin, Dion and The Belmonts, Duane Eddy, Jimmy Clanton and Jack Scott as the white acts; the black acts were Sil Austin and His Orchestra, The Olympics, Bobby Freeman, The Coasters, The Elegants,

51

The Danleers and Clyde McPhatter.

Sil Austin had a big all black orchestra, and they would play behind The Coasters or Bobby Freeman and play their hearts out. You let a white boy like Paul Anka, Bobby Darin, Jimmy Clanton or Frankie Avalon come out there, and they would kick the songs off real slow like they were trying to mess them up. We had our own group or band, but GAC had the singers singing with the orchestra. We had our own sound just like on the records, and the kids ate it up.

About the only thing in the movie, *The Buddy Holly Story* that was true was when he played the Apollo, they thought he was a black act when they

L to r: Carl Bunch in the background, Buddy Holly, Tommy Allsup.

booked him. That was an Alan Freed show; he booked Buddy when Buddy had three songs in the top ten, and Freed never did kick in any more money – it was sad how they used Buddy.

When the October tour was over Buddy returned to New York, and the two Crickets who had started out with him, Jerry Allison the drummer and Joe B. Mauldin the bass player, decided to go back and stay in Clovis with Norman Petty. Buddy was beginning to have a few hard feelings with Norman, but they decided to stay with Petty. I went to Odessa, Texas.

Moon Mullican was at the Silver Saddle Club that he and I had opened; we had been there off and on for several months, so I took the band back. It was the night before New Year's Eve, 1958, going into '59 and Buddy showed up at the club – he and a kid named Ray Rush who was a singer in the Roses. He said, "I want to tell you about this tour coming up". Another reason he was there was Buddy loved Moon Mullican. Our drummer was late, but we had to start the show. Buddy said, "Let me play drums". He pulled his glasses off and got back there; no one knew it was Buddy Holly. He played about an hour with us. Then the drummer rolled in, so Buddy and I talked. He told me about this tour coming up at the end of January.

He said "I've signed a new management contract with Irvin Feld, the President of General Artists Corporation (GAC)". Norman Petty had maintained control of Buddy's finances, so he had turned to Feld thinking that he could really help his career. He said, "We've got a tour coming up; Waylon will go along and play bass, can you get a drummer"? There was a little drummer who had been working around Odessa with Roy Orbison and some of the rock and roll bands, Carl Bunch. Buddy said that if he's any good bring him along. We were the last band Buddy Holly had – Tommy Allsup, Waylon Jennings and Carl Bunch.

53

Chapter 4
THE WINTER DANCE TOUR

"AT ALL OF THE SKATING/ROLLER RINKS BUDDY HOLLY
PLAYED IN TEXAS, HE WOULD START EACH SHOW WITH
'HEY, LET'S ROCK AND ROLL!' UNTIL BUDDY BECAME POPULAR,
THE MUSIC WAS RHYTHM AND BLUES".... *an anonymous fan*

We had been out for twelve miserably cold days on this tour, and the twelfth day was in Clear Lake, Iowa. We had played Green Bay, Wisconsin the night before and were on our way to Clear Lake. We had stopped on the way, and the Big Bopper had bought a sleeping bag. He said, "I'm gonna buy a sleeping bag 'cause I'm tired of freezin' on this bus". Buddy said, "I think I'm gonna charter a plane tonight and fly on up to Fargo". We were playing at Moorehead, Minnesota, the next night across the Red River from Fargo, North Dakota. If GAC had provided decent transportation, Buddy, the Bopper and Ritchie would not have been killed.

The tour was billed as The Winter Dance Party, and included not only Buddy Holly but also J. P. Richardson "The Big Bopper", Ritchie Valens, Dion and the Belmonts and Frankie Sardo. Jiles Perry Richardson, "The Big Bopper", was born in Sabine Pass, Texas in 1930, but grew up in Beaumont, Texas. After a stint in military service, he became a disc jockey in Beaumont, and since "The Bop" was the popular dance of the day he became "The Big Bopper" as a device to attract young listeners. He opened

Poster for the Thirty-fifth Anniversary of the Winter Dance Tour, Surf Ballroom, Clear Lake, Iowa.

his shows with "Hellooo Baby, it's the Big Bopper speakin". He wrote songs such as "White Lightning" recorded by George Jones and "Running Bear" made popular by Johnny Preston, but his primary recording success was "Chantilly Lace" that he cut in June 1958. It reached #6 in the charts and made Richardson a star who was welcomed into The Winter Dance Party tour.

Richard Steven Valenzuela was born in Pacoima, California in 1941, and soon showed musical talent. In 1958 he signed a contract with DEL-FI Records as possibly the first Hispanic or Latino rock and roll star, and for commercial advantage he became Ritchie Valens. His recording of an old Mexican wedding dance song "La Bamba" made him a star by late 1958. Ritchie Valens became a popular young seventeen year old member of The Winter Dance Party who potentially had a tremendous musical/ entertainment future.

Dion DiMucci was born in the Bronx, New York in 1939. He first recorded with a group he called the Timberlanes in 1957 on the Mohawk label; in 1958 he brought together three others and called themselves Dion and The Belmonts – the name Belmonts was taken from Belmont Avenue in the Bronx. Two of their recordings hit the charts in 1958 – "I Wonder Why" and "No One Knows". They were rising as a pop-rock and roll group when they joined the tour. Most of their top songs came after they were associated with the tour following the death of Buddy.

Frankie Sardo was the least known of the performers on the tour. He was born in Italy but grew up in New York. He became a pop-singer whose records never hit the charts. However, "Fake Out" on the ABC-Paramount label had earned a little popularity in the Midwest; thus, he was a member of the tour. It has been speculated that his father was a member of the syndicate that had interests in the entertainment business.

The original Crickets had left Buddy to work with Norman Petty, so Buddy went to his friend Tommy Allsup and requested that he once again tour with him and that he find a drummer. Buddy also purchased an electric bass for his friend Waylon Jennings to learn to play. Tommy recruited Carl Bunch an Odessa, Texas drummer who had been working with Roy Orbison and other young groups around West Texas. Tommy, Waylon and Carl caught a flight from Amarillo, Texas to New York, where Tommy worked at teaching Waylon to play the bass and where they rehearsed daily until the day to leave for Chicago – the starting gate for the Winter Dance Party tour.

The Chicago office of GAC was responsible for making all arrangements for the tour including transportation and housing; however, they were not responsible for the unbearable weather conditions. The first two weeks of the tour involved cris-crossing Wisconsin, Minnesota and Iowa – three states that had been hit hard by sub-zero temperature, heavy snow fall and numerous weather related deaths. When Buddy, Tommy, Waylon and Carl arrived by train in Chicago they were hit hard by the "below zero" atmosphere; wind chill was not reported in those days. Ritchie Valens had only worn a light jacket to wear on the tour; the performers who had been living in Texas and California were not prepared for the torture they were to endure. Not even the New York performers who were more acclimated for cold weather were ready for the winter of '59 .

On January 23, 1959 (Friday) they left Chicago for Milwaukee, Wisconsin and the Million Dollar Ballroom where it was reported close to 6,000 fans made dancing nearly impossible. From there they drove to Kenosha, Wisconsin and the Eagles Ballroom, and on Sunday, January 25 they had driven approximately 380 miles through snow and worsening conditions to Mankato, Minnesota. The next night they were in Eau Claire, Wisconsin; then they drove 240 miles westward back into Minnesota where they played the Fiesta Ballroom in Montevideo. The following day was January 28 and they had returned eastward to the Prom Ballroom in St. Paul, Minnesota. On the 29th they dropped down to Davenport, Iowa where it was a few degrees warmer than the upper states, but they had already experienced bus problems and bus replacement.

On Friday, January 30 as they headed toward Fort Dodge, Iowa and the Laramar Ballroom the heaters in the bus froze, and the Winter Dance Party troupe almost froze. The heaters had to be thawed in Tipton, Iowa before they could continue their trek. It was in Fort Dodge when Buddy seriously began to consider flying to the next gig, but to those who were licensed to fly it was too dangerous to attempt flying at night in sub-zero weather. From Fort Dodge they traveled to Duluth, Minnesota where it was twenty-four below zero and predicted to be thirty-five below. The musicians were getting short tempered from lack of rest and terrible travel conditions. On February 1, they were in Green Bay, Wisconsin and the Riverside Ballroom, and the tour continued to slide down hill. The next morning, February 2, they started their trip toward the Surf Ballroom in Clear Lake, Iowa some three hundred and forty miles away.

On February 2, 1959 when we got into Clear Lake, Iowa it was about 25 below zero. It was white. We had been up north for twelve days, and it was the same way everywhere. It was the cold time of the year for that part of the country. We were in Green Bay, Wisconsin the night before. We had been out for twelve days and had five different busses. The tour started out in Chicago, and the company that supplied the busses was sending out the old city busses that were broken down. The only warm night we had on that tour on the busses was when the bus broke down one night in some little old town, and we rented a school bus to go to the next job. That was the only bus that had a decent heater in it. It was rough ridin' for three hundred miles, but we stayed warm.

We played Clear Lake on the night of February 2. When we got to the Ballroom we probably didn't have an hour to set up, change and start playing. When we got there hundreds of kids were lined up, scuffling around, kicking their feet, for two or three blocks in that cold weather. How could they stand out there in twenty-five below weather – I couldn't even breath in it! I don't know how they did it. We had to put a scarf over our mouths just to go out to the bus, but I guess if you grow up in it you can handle it better.

Coming across northern Wisconsin we were going up a hill when the bus just completely stopped – it froze up. A car – sheriff's deputy out of Ironhead, Michigan – came along; he was going to a town back up the road. He took Carl Bunch, our drummer, whose feet had become frost bitten on the bus – we were burning paper in the aisle of the bus trying to keep warm. We said that this kid needed to get to the hospital, so we loaded him in the deputy's four wheel drive and took Carl back to that little town and put him in the hospital with frost bite. Carl rejoined us three days later; he missed Clear Lake. The next day we got a train down to Green Bay; we had a show that afternoon in another little town (Appleton, Wisconsin) that we had to cancel. We checked into a hotel and went to the concert that night in taxis. I think it was colder there than anywhere else. It was there where a clerk in the hotel said, "You guys put something over your mouths when you step out there to get in the cabs".

I swear the kids were lined up for blocks at the Riverside Ballroom in Green Bay; it was estimated that there were over 2,000 kids waiting to see and hear Buddy. There we had a drummer from a little local band to sit in with us, but Buddy and Ritchie could play drums and Carlos of Dion and the Belmonts could play drums. So when Ritchie sang Buddy played drums, and when Buddy performed that night Ritchie Valens came out and played drums for Buddy Holly. You know, stars in this day and age would never think about going out and backing up a fellow star.

So when we got to Clear Lake, Iowa we really didn't have a drummer except for the stars. Waylon and I set up Carl's drums and started. I think one of the Belmonts played behind a kid named Frankie Sardo. Then the Big Bopper would come out, and I believe one of the Belmonts played behind him; then Buddy or Ritchie would play behind the Belmonts, then they would back up each other playing drums. That's what happened in Clear Lake. The Belmonts didn't sing harmony with Buddy; Waylon and I sang his harmony. We opened each of our shows with Billy Grammer's "Gotta Travel On"; that was our first number. Buddy liked that number, and it had just been a hit. We were sort of a country rockabilly group when we played that song. That was the first hit on the Monument label; Billy Grammer's hit started the label.

The Buddy Holly portion of the show was the closing portion. After they were killed, Waylon and I still opened with that song. Then Waylon would sing some of Buddy's songs. I knew Waylon was going to be a star because the kids went crazy over him. They would scream and holler when he sang; it was written on the wind that he was destined to become a star. He did Buddy's songs the first couple of nights, and then we got a kid from Odessa, Ronnie Smith, a rock and roll singer I knew. He helped us in the last couple of weeks of the tour. Waylon would still do his share of them. GAC promised to pay us so much if we finished the tour. Frankie Avalon came along to do some of the shows, and Jimmy Clanton did some. I think Frankie finished the tour with us. We did the Fargo show with just Dion and the Belmonts, Waylon and me, and Bobby Vee had a little band up there before he ever started recording. We had a night off, and they brought in Frankie Avalon and a couple other acts to finish the tour.

The Belmonts were nuts. We stopped one night, and one of them bought a pistol. We were going down the road on the bus, and he was sitting across the aisle from me with that pistol, aiming it and going "pow" and saying, "I got the driver; pow, I got the Big Bopper". I said, "Man, you shouldn't be doing that, it might be loaded". He said, "Don't worry, I took all of the shells out of it". He said, "We used to make zip guns". I said, "What is a zip gun"? He said that they made them out of a clothes pin, a rubber band and a piece of pipe. The zip gun was born up in the Bronx. Dion never used his last name; he was always Dion and recorded as Dion.

It was around the midnight hour; it was a pretty long show, probably 9 to 12. They took off around 2 a. m. They weren't that far from the airport when they went down. They have never found out what caused the crash. It had been snowing, but *it was clear when they took off.* They didn't find them until 9:30 the next morning.

That day on the way to Clear Lake the Bopper bought his sleeping bag, and Buddy went to a pay phone and called Clovis. He had a CPA in Clovis going over Norman Petty's books. I was sitting on the bus, and Buddy got back on madder than hell. He said, "You're not goin' to believe this, but I don't have any money in any bank in Clovis. I thought I had about $50,000 in the bank". If he had, $25,000 would have been his and the other $25,000 split between Joe B. and Jerry. They were living out there at that time with Petty, but Buddy didn't know what had happened to the money. He said, "When this tour is over, we're goin' to Clovis and I'm goin' to get my money, if I have to take it out of Norman's hide. I'm goin' to get my money. I'm goin' to kick his ass, and take a leak on his fireplace".

Norman had a sitting room where the fireplace was in his apartment in the back of his studio; we would all go back and sit, and he would always say, "Don't put anything in the fireplace; no smoking and no

61

Cokes on it". They were more particular about the fireplace than they were about the controls in the studio. Buddy said, "I'm goin' to stand right in front of that fireplace and take a leak in the middle of it, and if Norman says anything, I'm goin' to kick his ass and Vi's, too". He was mad. "I'm goin' to get my money, one way or the other, because I know it's there". He was disappointed, heart broken and mad. Norman Petty's estate now is in the hands of some attorneys in Clovis.

I had a pistol and sold it to Buddy for twenty-five dollars – a twenty-two revolver type that today is called a midnight special. He kept it in his briefcase and carried it in his car. They found it when the plane crashed. I sold it to him during the summer tour when he was carrying all of that money. The summer tour was the original Crickets plus the dance band that he had me put together with friends from Oklahoma City. The fall tour was the original Crickets with me plus Petty's background singing and staff group The Roses; they had had a record release prior to that tour. They sang background on some of Buddy's songs.

When we got into Clear Lake the guy who owned the Surf Ballroom said, "Dwyer Flying Service has a charter service here in Clear Lake, I'll call them". He did, and it cost $112 for three guys to fly four hundred miles in a Beechcraft Bonanza. Buddy, Waylon and I were to fly. Well, when the Big Bopper heard about it, he kinda had the flu and talked Waylon out of his seat. Sometime while we were setting up to play that night Ritchie Valens heard about it; he came and asked me if he could fly in my place, and I said "No". He asked me three or four times if he could fly during the night.

After the show that night, this station wagon pulled up to the back door of the stage and Buddy and the Big Bopper were in the station wagon along with Mr. Anderson who owned the Surf Ballroom; he was taking them to the airport. I went to the bus where I had a little satchel that I put all my dirty white shirts in that needed cleaning; then I went to the station wagon and opened the back door and set it in there. Buddy was in the front seat with the driver, and the Bopper was in the second seat. Buddy said, "Tommy, you better make sure we've got every thing loaded". Back in those days we didn't have roadies. I went back in there, and when you go in the back door of the Surf Ballroom there's a dressing room and to your left the stage – you go up four or five steps. You go through the dressing room, and there's a door that goes to the dance floor. Ritchie was standing there in that doorway signing autographs. I went back in, and he said, "Hey, let me go", and I said, "No". He said, "I've never flown in a little plane; let me try it".

For some reason, I reached in my pocket and pulled out a half dollar and said, "Call it". He said, "Heads". It fell on the floor – it was heads! I said, "You're flying". His eyes lit up, and I went back to the station wagon and said, "Buddy, I'm not going on the plane". He said, "How come"? I said, "Me and Ritchie just flipped a coin, and he's goin' in my place". In the movie they show it happened at the airport, but this is the way it happened. I said to Buddy, "My mother sent me a letter that will be at the Fargo post office and there's a check in it". I had gotten an income tax return or something; "Will you go pick it up for me"? I didn't know if we would get there in time in that broken down bus for me to get it. He said, "Yeh, give me some identification". I pulled out my driver's license and he said, "Just give me your wallet". He just took my wallet and stuck it in his inside coat pocket. The next morning when they found that crash, they found four bodies and five identifications. Ritchie's clothes were almost torn off of him. I think Buddy's coat was ripped, but when the first news went out they had me listed as being on the plane. They couldn't figure out why there were five identifications but only four bodies. The pilot's name was Roger Peterson; *that's how the flip of the coin* came about. Mr. Anderson identified the bodies, and told them that I wasn't on the plane.

When we got to Fargo about 11:00 in the next morning (they found the bodies about 9:30), Sam Geller, who was the road manager, and I walked into the hotel. At the edge of the lobby was a television with a picture of the Big Bopper on it at that particular moment. We walked over to the desk and said that we had reservations – that we were the band for the traveling road show. And I said, "Put me in a room next to Buddy Holly". The desk man said, "But Buddy Holly is dead". I said, "What"! He said, "Buddy Holly was killed in a plane crash – Buddy Holly, Ritchie Valens and the Big Bopper were killed this morning". When I looked back over at the television, it was showing Buddy or Ritchie, one of them. That's how we found out about it.

I went back out to the bus and Waylon was getting up about that time. He had been back there asleep, and everybody was beginning to wake up. I went back to Waylon and said, "You aren't goin' to believe this – Buddy is dead – he got killed in a plane crash". We went into the hotel and checked into a room. I called my mother; she lived in Claremore, and I said, "Have you had your television on this morning"? She said, "No, I've been working around the house and haven't turned it on". While I was talking to her, a neighbor lady was trying to call her to tell her that I had been killed in a plane crash. After I hung up she called again and said that the line had been busy. I headed that call off which was a weird coincidence.

Why did the two Crickets quit? *Buddy was the Crickets.* Joe B. didn't really play on many of the records; they used other bass players. Jerry was a great rock and roll drummer and helped him write a lot of songs. I think that the fact that Buddy had married a Puerto Rican and wanted to live in New York was part of the problem. They wanted to live in Texas, and Buddy was trying to break it off with Petty. Norman influenced Joe B. and Jerry by saying, "Stay out here, and we'll form a new Crickets". Which they did. They added Sonny Curtis and Earl Sinks and made a record; at the end of that last tour they were there to meet us in New York City. We (Waylon, Carl, me) had this big meeting at GAC, who at that time were the only ones booking rock and roll; GAC said that the only way they would book the Crickets would be if "Tommy" was a part of it. That meant that they would have to send Sonny back to Texas. So four went back to Lubbock, and four stayed in New York.

I felt real bad about it because I knew that the name "The Crickets" wouldn't be successful because Buddy Holly had been on Decca Records. He had gone to Nashville and recorded four sides with Owen Bradley; they were released but nothing happened, so Paul Cohen dropped Buddy from Decca. Norman Petty cut "That'll Be The Day" took it up to New York and played it for the people at Coral, which was owned by Decca; they said, "Those guys are great; who are they"? Norman said, "It's a group called The Crickets". They released The Crickets on their Brunswick label which they reactivated for "rock and roll" and The Crickets. It became number one on the charts. Norman took "Peggy Sue" to them, and they said, "Who's that singing". He said, "Buddy Holly". They replied, "We can't sign Buddy Holly because we dropped him". Norman said, "You've already signed him; *he's The Crickets*". Probably to save face they put out "Peggy Sue" on Coral Records, and it goes to the top ten. The back side of "That'll Be The Day" is "Oh, Boy", and it was climbing the charts. They had three songs in the top ten at the same time. Buddy Holly could do just about what he wanted to do with Decca and

Coral and the powers that be. That's how The Crickets came about, so I figured that when Buddy was killed, The Crickets went with him.

There's a story that surfaced saying that Buddy called the original Crickets to come back, but he didn't. And there's another story that that night he was trying to get through to them, and they called the Surf but couldn't get through to him. I don't think he would ever have gone back to what he was doing. It seems that the Petty thing split every thing up. They stayed with Petty; they were with Petty the day Buddy got killed. He died thinking that those guys were with Petty, so I don't think he called them to come back. He would have said something to me, but it makes good press for them to say that he was calling. When Buddy got killed that was the end of The Crickets; **BUDDY HOLLY WAS THE CRICKETS!** It was just a name. He was the one who sang "That'll Be The Day"; it wasn't The Crickets. They really didn't sing on anything; The Tolletts sang the background on the record, not Jerry and Joe B. It was Buddy's way of getting a record produced. We stayed in New York about four weeks after he was killed; that was the longest four weeks of my life, being in New York City with nothing to do. We did a couple of television shows; the booking agency could not get any bookings because nobody wanted to see The Crickets without Buddy Holly. I told them it would be that way, but they didn't believe me. So I said, "Boys, I'm going back to Odessa; I've got a job back there".

People have often asked me, "What kind of person was Buddy Holly"? We talked a lot, and he was really a serious person. He thought a lot and was full of ideas. He had a lot of things he wanted to do. We were going to come back to Lubbock and build a recording studio and a music store. He wanted his dad to run the store, and he wanted his two brothers to be involved in his music. He made a deal with Coral to give him so much front money for masters of anyone we found who might be good enough to be recorded. He had to take them in the studio and cut a demo and send it to Coral. It was an independent production deal that he already had made. That's what soured me on Lubbock – they waited so long to do anything for him. He did not abandon Lubbock as some people say. He had every intention in the world to go back to Lubbock. He was going to have a publishing company, a production company, a record store, a label, a music store – his whole music business right there in Lubbock. **Buddy Holly put Lubbock, Texas on the map!**

He was quiet; he wasn't a drinker or into drugs. On that last tour, he was a solemn type person. He was real happy with his new management in New York City. He thought he had about fifty grand in the bank in Clovis, but when we started that last tour he was broke. He had people in Clovis going over the books, and they couldn't find any money for him. He died without knowing what Norman Petty did with his money; however, a church in Clovis had a new sound system and organ donated in Buddy's name by Norman Petty. Buddy never had a bank account for all of the money he made from shows and recordings with Norman Petty; the money went to a bank account, and Petty wrote checks on it. If Buddy wanted something he bought it with a credit card, and Petty sent the check for it.

That summer, the first tour I made with him, he had a Lincoln; I rode with him, Jerry and Joe B. I was older and had more experience in music and road work, so Norman told me, "Tommy when you check out at night hold out the band money and send the rest to Clovis, and we'll put it Buddy's account". We didn't send one receipt to Norman; Buddy took the cash, paid the band and put the rest in the car glove box. We'd be driving down the road and Jerry would say, "Buddy, I need some money". Buddy would reach into the glove box and pull out a hand full of money and sling it into the back seat. He had never handled his own money up to that point and was like a kid in a toy shop. He had made a lot of bread, but didn't get to enjoy it as much as others did.

He was broke when we started that last tour. After he was killed GAC told Waylon and me, "You know the old adage - the show must go on; if you and Waylon leave, the show is going to fold and there's no way back to Lubbock". We were basically snowed in up north; they said, "We'll give you the same thing we were paying Buddy", which was a lot of money for that day and time – not much today. We said, "OK". But when we got back to New York City those rascals said that they had advanced Buddy money for the tour and that his wife got some money to go to Lubbock when he got killed, so he was overdrawn. I said, "Well, what about the train tickets I bought to get us back to New York"? They said, "Well, we'll reimburse you for your travel". And that's all we got except for our salaries. So I wasn't real happy about hanging around New York City.

When I did that first session with Buddy, Norman showed me a check from the record company that was $87,000 – his first royalty payment on "Peggy Sue" and "That'll Be The Day". That was 1958 and was like a million dollars today. On the copyright of "Peggy Sue", it says Jerry Allison and Norman Petty. Buddy wrote "Cindy Lou", but when they recorded it the first time it didn't sound right. Jerry Allison said, "I've got this girl friend in Lubbock named Peggy Sue". They switched it. Maybe Jerry helped him write it, but *it is Buddy's song*.

We made a tape or two in his apartment the night before that last tour; he had written six new songs: "Peggy Sue Got Married", "That Makes It Tough", "Crying, Waiting, Hoping", "What To Do", "Learning The Game" and "That's What They Say". In the apartment session I played the guitar on a couple of songs; he played guitar, and I played bass on a couple. He had the old original mono Ampex recorder that Norman Petty had used to record "That'll Be The Day". The cabinet model was like a suitcase Ampex. We put those songs on it.

I played lead on "Wishing". Just before we did the summer tour, Bobby Darin had this "Early In The Morning" song, and Buddy went in the studio and covered him. It hit the charts in August, 1958 just before we did the October tour. He ate Darin's lunch with that song. He had three black ladies singing backup vocals, and they were honking. They had George Barnes on guitar, Panama Francis playing drums and other excellent musicians. They cut it live at the Pythian Temple in New York City. They did that one song and rushed it right out.

Alan Freed, the disc jockey who got banned from radio in Boston for playing rock and roll, had this big rock and roll package put together. Buddy told me that during that late 1957 tour he was on the bus trying to sleep, and Laverne Baker had been harassing everybody on the bus. He woke up, and she was right in his face with her fingers just like she was going to pounce on him. He had a little 22 pistol (not the one I sold him), pulled it and said, "I'm gonna blow your goddamn head off if you don't get the hell out of here". He said that he was really mad at them because they had played Chicago, and in the hotel where they had stayed Laverne Baker and Ruth Brown had gotten someone down in the basement, took all his clothes off and put Vaseline all over him – tore open some pillows and put feathers on him and locked him out in the hallway. Holly was kind of mad about that. He was a regular kind of person who said, "I'm from Texas and you don't jack with me". He respected black artists like Fats Domino and Little Richard, but he didn't want anyone to jack him around.

During that Autumn, 1958 tour we did a show in Norfolk, Virginia, and they had reservations for us at a hotel where they wouldn't let the black acts stay. They had to go back over across town. The next night when we did our show we went back to the dressing room, and they had taken all of our clothes out of our hangup bags – our shirts – and had polished their shoes with our white shirts. Our shirts had shoe polish all over them. They really messed up our clothes bad. Come to find out, it was one of the black singing groups, a group that had only one hit. It really pissed Buddy off. Most of the black groups we got along with fine, but two or three of the vocal groups that had only one hit were complete ass holes. I said that once in an interview, and it was published in 1974 or '75 and some little chick picked it up in Europe and said that I said that black groups were ass holes. She wanted me to make a public apology and send it back to her. I should have written something back, but I just threw it away.

On the Autumn show Frankie Avalon, Duane Eddy, Jimmy Clanton, Dion and The Belmonts and Bobby Darin were with us all the way; Jack Scott quit the tour in Canada – he was thinking about his girlfriend. He just quit; I produced him in later years. We had our own cars on that tour, and there were two buses. Every now and then we would let Eddy and others ride with us just to give them a break. There was a seventeen piece orchestra, and each group might have five or six men. Buddy had his wife with him and drove his car; Jerry, Joe B. and I had a station wagon pulling the instrument trailer. Clyde McPhatter, one of the black entertainers from New York, had a big Cadillac that he drove.

On the Summer Tour that we made Buddy was still single. He didn't drink a lot, maybe every now and then he might have a beer. He just wasn't a heavy drinker. The October Tour we did, Maria Elena was with him, and they drove in his car. He got a speeding ticket going through South Carolina in one of those speed traps. I was right behind him. We had a new DeSoto station wagon and a trailer, and he had a '58 Cadillac. We were burning up the road; everybody else was on the buses. We were driving probably about 80, and got pulled over. They took us right down to the justice of the peace. He said, "You follow me". Each car was fifty dollars. Buddy peeled off a hundred dollar bill off a roll of hundreds, and said, "I hope you sons a bitches enjoy this, 'cause you need it a lot more than I do". I thought "Oh, Oh, we're headed to jail"! That's the only time I saw him really mad except when he said that he was going to piss on Petty's fireplace.

I've had thousands of people ask me about the toss of the coin, and then, "... now tell me the significance of Buddy Holly". Until he got killed it was just a job, other than I really liked working for him. The money was good, and we stayed in better hotels than with the Wills. And we had bigger crowds. I was "western swing" in a "rock and roll" world. It was different. It was like your parents – until they pass away; each year they get a little smarter than they were when you were a kid. Since Buddy's death, it seems that he has gotten better; his songs are still holding up today. He was way ahead of the performers and shows of today. He had it all together. He knew exactly what he wanted on his recordings, and he wrote all of his songs. There are other peoples' names on them, *but he wrote them*. They were his ideas. What we did on records every little band could do. These little bands would start up, but we were sort of the first step up in their music.

They would learn what we were doing instead of copying a group like Chicago. It was the simplicity of it – the simplicity of his songs and style that made him last all through the years. You listened to Buddy Holly's songs; there are no theatrics. Garage bands were usually two guitars, drums and an electric bass. That was the nucleus of rock and roll – two guitars, drums and an electric bass. I feel like we had a big hand in it because of what we were recording. I probably cut ten or twelve records in Norman Petty's studio. We did six up in Buddy's apartment in NYC. Now they've taken all the music off them and put them in their original form with Buddy the way they should be. There are a couple with my guitar on them.

I want to stress *that Buddy Holly was coming back to Lubbock and that Norman Petty did not write all those songs.* I just know what Buddy told me. Irvin Feld, the president of GAC (General Artist Corporation in New York City), had purchased the Ringling Circus, and later became a legitimate theater promoter. They reimbursed us for our tickets from Chicago to New York City, but they didn't pay us for the extra amount above our salary that we were supposed to have gotten for finishing the tour for Buddy. We had practiced Buddy's songs in New York – Carl, Waylon, and I – and when we got to Chicago we had the songs down pretty good. I had taught the songs to Waylon on bass. When we got to Chicago, we found out that we were going to back up everybody. It was kinda a surprise. So we had to learn all of Ritchie's songs and the Big Bopper's, Frankie Sardo and Dion and the Belmonts. We thought they were going to send a band along on the tour; all they did was send a couple of horn players, a sax player and a trumpet player, that was it, and they only backed up Frankie Sardo. The sax may have backed up the Big Bopper, but Waylon, Carl and I backed up all the acts.

Ritchie played his own lead. He did his own guitar work on "La Bamba" and a few rock and roll numbers. He was going to be a pretty good rock and roll guitar player. I played rhythm behind him, and he would ask how I was playing chords. He wanted to learn. We weren't paid anything extra for backing up everybody. It was one of those brother-in-law deals. In those days when you left the big cities the musicians union was very weak. I don't know what the horn players were making, but Waylon and I were probably being paid a little more. On that tour I was making $250 a week and Waylon was getting $200. In his book it says a little more, but this is what we were making. Bunch was getting a little less than Waylon. Later Carl kicked around a little and played with Hank Williams, Jr. when he was starting up in the '60s, but he is in the ministry now. I didn't talk to him from '63 or '64 when I was with Liberty Records until September, 1999 when they opened the Buddy Holly Center in Lubbock.

In his third book, *Waylon: An Autobiography* (New York: Warner Books, 1996) Waylon said things about me that aren't true, and his narrative leaves the impression that I wasn't there most of the time. I'm going to be real nice about him because Waylon and I have been good friends; I believe the writer put things in to spice it up. There are mistakes in his book that I want to clear up, and he contradicts himself in this last one when contrasted to the first two books. He states that Buddy talked to him all the time; Buddy didn't say much to Waylon on that whole tour, but he talked to me a lot about opening that studio in Lubbock. On the stage every now and then he would tell Waylon to turn the bass down – it was too loud. In one book Waylon said that I helped him on the bass and stayed on his ass, and I probably did stay on him trying to get him to play it right. You know, I try to say nice things about people.

Buddy got acquainted with Waylon on KLLL Radio in Lubbock; High Pockets Duncan, a popular Lubbock disc jockey, introduced them. Waylon was a disc jockey part-time on KLLL. In the summer of 1958,

Buddy told me that there was a friend of his in Lubbock on KLLL that he wanted to cut a couple of sides on. We did on September 10, 1958; we cut "Jole Blon" and "When Sin Stops". He brought in the great tenor saxophone player King Curtis for a song he was going to cut and also used him in Waylon's session; I'm not mentioned as being at the session, but I played rhythm guitar on it. Right after that session Buddy was gone; he was married and went on a long extended honeymoon to South America. When he came back we made the October tour around the East Coast. After that tour Buddy moved to New York. Apparently, when Buddy was in Lubbock during the holidays and came to see me in Odessa, he cut one song at the KLLL studios with Waylon and one of the station owners clapping their hands in the background.

When Waylon, Carl and I went to New York in early January, 1959 we drove to Amarillo and flew to Chicago and then got a flight to New York. There is a mistake in Waylon's book; we got the flight the night before it crashed into the East River in New York City. He tells that it crashed somewhere, but it crashed in the East River at Laguardia – they should have done their research. It just didn't make the end of the runway.

It's like other things that he claimed were said. He claimed that Buddy said, "I hope your old bus freezes" and that he said, "Well, I hope your old plane crashes" (p. 57). These comments surfaced thirty-five years after the fact. These are stories he dreamed or his writer dreamed. Some say Paul Anka was on the tour; he was never near the tour. The only thing about Paul is that he had written a song, "It Doesn't Matter Anymore" that Buddy had out. Waylon said that Buddy called what he was doing "Western and Bop" (p.48). No! *Buddy called it "Rock and Roll"*. Buddy had tried country/western, and it didn't work for him. He told me that he didn't like it; he didn't dislike it, but "it's not my preference". He tried, but didn't like the steel guitar. He liked Hank Williams and George Jones' "White Lightnin'". He liked Billy Grammer's version of "Gotta Travel On". It was a rockabilly type of record without the steel guitar. He liked Elvis Presley, Bill Haley, Little Richard, Fats Domino. He didn't dislike Bob Wills and Hank Thompson, but he said that they were not his preference.

When Buddy was producing Waylon, indeed, Waylon probably felt uncomfortable in the studio; it was Norman's way that made Waylon feel unwelcome. Norman stayed behind the console and hardly ever came out. Waylon said that Buddy pitched him an electric bass, and said, "You have two weeks to learn to play that thing" (p. 56). That was before the tour. Buddy may have left a bass with him in Lubbock; I don't know. But we didn't practice until we got to New York City, and in his latest book, Waylon doesn't mention that I'm the one who taught him to play the bass. We rehearsed Buddy's songs, and when we got to Chicago, we rehearsed the other guys' songs. Waylon was having trouble because he had never played bass. I told him to think of it as the lower strings on the guitar; the bass is a fairly easy instrument for a guitar player to play.

We both stayed with Buddy; Carl stayed in a hotel room. I think Waylon was only there one night; he has it wrong (p. 57). Maria Elena told me that she only remembered Waylon being there the last night before we left on the tour. Waylon stated that Maria Elena wasn't a good cook (p. 57), but she was a great cook. She fixed breakfast for us each morning, and she cooked Spanish style chicken – it was great. And he said that she didn't speak English very well, but she spoke well enough to run a publishing company in New York – Southern Music. She spoke English very well. Buddy had the recorder that Norman had used to record "That'll Be The Day". We were constantly messing around recording, and he was constantly putting down stuff while we were there.

Waylon said that I played the bass on some of those, but I played the guitar. He said that we ate liverwurst (p.58); I hate liverwurst. We went to the Stagedoor Deli and had pastrami on rye. After the plane crash, while I was up there with the Crickets, we lived on pastrami on rye. At least it is where the Stagedoor Deli is now; it may not have been named that then.

Buddy had an old Gibson guitar that had leather on it, not a new Gibson (p. 59) . I didn't smoke in those days, and *I don't remember Buddy smoking.* There is a photo of Waylon and Buddy that was taken in one of the twenty-five cent photo machines; it recently surfaced, but I don't know that it shows Buddy smoking. We all made photos in those machines; we were killing time at the train depot. Frankie Sardo wasn't a great singer, but he was good enough to get a recording contract with a New York company. We thought he was with the Mafia. I'm not sure that Chicago is where Frankie Sardo's father showed up (p.61); our show there was disrupted. We were backing Frankie Avalon at the Aragon Ballroom; there was an orchestra pit in front of the big stage, and we were on the big stage. Police were ringed around the orchestra pit, but the kids pushed past the cops and started up on the stage. The little guy who owned the Aragon came screaming out "Close the curtains! Close the curtains! They're tearing up my ballroom"! They took us back and locked us in some dressing rooms. When we finally came out there were two or three girls passed out on stretchers; they fainted when they saw Frankie Avalon. I remember that Sardo's father showed up, but it could have been in Milwaukee; Sardo did have a good sense of humor and was the Bobby Darin type.

On the bus we were trying to stay warm, and the Belmonts were burning paper to stay warm until the driver made them put it out. Waylon said that one morning Buddy woke him and asked if he wanted to go to

England, not to mention it to Tommy (p. 64). But the England tour was already booked before we left New York. We knew that when we finished this tour we had six weeks off and then a two weeks European tour already booked. That came with the new management.

Waylon states that Ritchie and I were across the room flipping a coin to see who would fly; in the book it says "Tommy called tails and lost" (p. 67). He wasn't even around when I flipped the coin, and, as previously told, it was Ritchie who made the call and won, but lost.

When we got to Fargo, Waylon said that Sam Geller, the tour manager, woke him (p. 68). No, Waylon was still asleep when I came back out and woke him. The tour manager did not come back to the bus. I did. And GAC did not offer to fly us back to the funeral (p. 69); all they said was that we should finish the tour. I had talked to one of Buddy's brothers who was going to fly up for the body, and according to him it was going to be a closed casket funeral. But GAC – they didn't even pay our train tickets much less fly us back for the funeral; they wanted us to keep the tour going. I talked to Irving Feld, and he said, "You know the show must go on". I don't like funerals; I probably wouldn't have gone if I had been there.

Bill Parsons sang "The All-American Boy", and he worked with us maybe two days – maybe a weekend. That was the name of the song that Bobby Bare had out; Bobby got drafted, so they put Bill Parsons on the road as the hit singer promoting the record as his. They were two different people; Bobby Bare was not Bill Parsons (p. 70). I know them both. Fraternity Records put that information out later because they had skimmed the people. Bobby had the demo that they released as a record, but Parsons was the one on the road.

I was never jealous of Waylon; I had no reason to be, and we did get along (p. 71). However, he may have been a little envious after Buddy died, but I helped him get a job on KYOL Radio in Odessa. He came down and worked a while, and then I didn't see him for twenty years. I saw him in Lubbock in 1979. I always thought that he would do well. Yes, I sent for the Elvis looking singer, Ronnie Smith (p. 71). He was in Odessa, and Carl Bunch had been working with him. I had recorded with him in Clovis with the Pettys. He was good, and at the time Waylon was jealous of him. While Buddy was alive, I basically acted as his road manager; he would give me the money, and I would pay Carl and Waylon. I was older and more experienced than they were, and after Buddy was killed I paid them. I also had to wire money to the hospital where Carl was for him to fly down to meet us. At that point I was calling the songs and leading the band, and that's probably why Waylon thought that I didn't like him. I insisted that Ronnie sing half of the songs, but Waylon really did more than he. Ronnie played rhythm guitar and was a good singer. He was like Elvis, and the kids loved him – but he got on drugs. Waylon got on drugs much later, not on our tour, and *I did not put pills in his drink on the way back to Chicago!*

Chapter 5
L. A. TURN AROUNDS

There were no drugs until after Buddy got killed, and Ronnie Smith came on the tour. He had been down to Del Rio and bought a bottle of those white cross Benzedrine pills – the ones called L. A. Turn Arounds – real bennies. You could take one in New York and drive to Los Angeles and turn around and drive back.

The last night of the Winter Dance Tour Ronnie was taking pills, and Waylon was drinking. Waylon would say, "Ronnie, you shouldn't take those pills; they're not good for you". Ronnie would say, "Waylon, you shouldn't drink and get drunk every night 'cause it's bad for you". This went on for about ten days; so the last night of the tour we were going back to Chicago from Peoria, Illinois. Waylon had some vodka in a Seven-Up bottle, and I said, "Give me a drink of your vodka". He was in the seat in front of me. There was a chick on the tour he had been moving in on – pretty good gal singer – a good looking gal married to someone in the business. He just handed the Seven-Up back to me. I was behind him and Ronnie Smith was in the next seat. Ronnie reached up and got the Seven-Up, pulled it back there and took two or three of his pills, crumbled them up and put them in Waylon's Seven-Up and then handed it back to him. I wasn't going to drink it 'cause I didn't want to stay up for a week. Waylon still thinks I did it, but I didn't – it was Ronnie Smith. Ronnie later became addicted to glue sniffing; it did something to his brain. I think he did it out of rejection. He tried so hard to be a star and never made it. He was one of those good looking boys who looked like Elvis Presley and tried hard to make it, but never got the right breaks. His family put him in a state hospital for treatment, but it didn't work. He committed suicide in 1962.

We got back to Chicago about two in the morning. The bus let us off at the train depot, Central Station. Across the street from the depot was one of those three dollars a night flop houses. Waylon said, "Me and the chick are goin' over and get us a room". We had about four hours before the train was to leave for New York. About five thirty here comes Waylon really pissed off; he said, "Man I don't know what happened; we got in bed and nothing happened. That's never happened to me in my life". Well, those pills will do that to you. I had taken some before, and I knew what they would do.

We got on the train headed for New York. We had already been up one night; we're in the section where you can lay back a little bit in the seats. I said, "Sit down". He said, "No, I want to walk around a little bit". He started walking like a greased lighting bolt. The further we got out of Chicago, the faster he was walking. Those pills had really kicked in. All day long, we'd say, "Eat something". He'd say, "Naw, I'll drink some coffee". You don't drink coffee after you've had bennies, because you'll just react to it again. Poor Waylon walked all day, all night and the next day. We got in New York at 6 o'clock in the evening, and we were supposed to check in to some hotel they had us booked in. We had a meeting the next day with GAC and Norman Petty. We got a cab and went to the hotel. I got us two rooms, and said, "Waylon, you goin' ta bed"? He said, "Naw, I'm too excited; I'm gonna walk around a little bit". Back in those days you could walk around 42nd and Times Square. We go to bed, and about 3 o'clock – this is the third night he's been awake – and I hear a knock. I go to the door, and Waylon's eyes look like two piss holes in the snow. He said, "Man, I'm tired; I've got to lay down and sleep". He went to bed, and we had that meeting the next morning at ten o'clock. He was worn out, but he made the meeting with us. Those suckers wouldn't pay us. They just barely paid us for our train tickets. That's when they told us Buddy owed them a lot of money – **they were rotten men.**

Waylon has had two or three biographies written, and his story is different in each. In one he says that a guy on the tour slipped pills in his drink. In one he says that Tommy and Ronnie did it, and in the last one he accuses me for getting him started on pills (p. 71). To set the record straight, my hands never touched those pills. But I was there, and I knew exactly what was going to happen when he drank it. I've told him what happened, but he still believes that I did it. I told people years ago that he was going to be a star someday. He could sing, and even though our crowds were built in, I saw them react to him. Waylon wouldn't go back to play Clear Lake until 1996, the thirty-seventh anniversary; he took his band and played a show. I went back for the thirty-fifth. He did hire The Crickets to tour with him back in the mid-80s and has recorded a tribute to Buddy.

As previously stated, Buddy had produced a session on Waylon; we did the session at Petty's. It came out on Coral later, but nothing happened with it. Waylon had never played a bass before, and I had to teach him. I said, "Just think of the last four strings on a guitar - G D A E". And I had to teach him the songs. He'd get carried away and play loud. We were friends – I'd go my way and he'd go his way. He didn't talk about Buddy much. I think it spooked him a little more than it did me; he was really let down. It hurt him and probably set his career back a little 'cause Buddy probably would have done some more sessions with him. His popularity might have been five or ten years sooner if Buddy hadn't been killed. You never know. But Buddy thought Waylon had something special.

Like I said I knew what those pills, "White Crosses", that Ronnie slipped him would do, because I had an earlier experience with them. I tried one down on North Main in Tulsa. Paul McGhee and I went in to see Judge McNally, who had been a horn player in the Texas Playboys; I was seventeen or eighteen and Paul was a year or two older, probably in 1949. We had our little band. The Judge was playing in a little club down near the viaduct. We went by to see him, and he said, "Do you guys want to get high"? Paul said, "Why not"? Judge had liquid Benzedrine; in those days you could buy it in nose drops. They finally outlawed it. You could put a drop in your nose and sniff it up, or you could put a drop in a Seven-Up, which I did, and went home and looked at the ceiling. I heard a rooster crowing the next morning and got up. My dad and mom were making coffee; Paul came by and we jammed all day, went out that night and played a job. I came home that night and looked at the ceiling again. I didn't close my eyes for about three days, and I told Paul that I didn't ever want anymore of that stuff. He said, "It is pretty potent, isn't it". It kept me awake for two nights, and those little white pills did the same thing.

The song "Six Days on the Road" says that with little white pills my eyes are open wide. Women have been taking them for diet pills for fifty years. It curbs your appetite; they are not as strong now. Back then, *the "bennies" were strong.* Musicians had to drive three or four hundred miles to a job night after night and took them to stay awake. Now days people say, "We took a pill to lose weight" and think nothing about it. Lloyd Jordon, a bass player still working with us, would go down and buy salt pills; they had a cross on them. They looked just like the "bennies". We would be playing a dance and Lloyd would take one out and purposely lay it maybe on the piano, and some of the musicians

82

who really liked them would see it and take it. They thought they had "bennies"; I've seen two or three of them take those salt pills thinking they were "bennies" and get high. We would just laugh. I never did get into the drugs, because I've seen too many men who got their lives screwed up with them. I smoked a little pot a time or two, and all it did for me was make me sleepy.

In 1976 Jesse Ashlock told me at the Austin City Limits show that he had cancer; we were worried about him, but it was Sleepy Johnson who died during those sessions. Jesse asked me if I had ever smoked any "weed". I said that it didn't do anything for me, and he said that since he had cancer, he smoked a little each night before going to bed. He said that he couldn't sleep because the cancer was eating on him, so he smoked a little to help him sleep. He had a prescription for it. I don't believe that Bob or Johnnie Lee ever had any problems with band members being on drugs. The biggest thing with drugs in the early days was a few would smoke grass. They didn't abuse it, because *they didn't have the money to abuse it.* Usually somebody gave them some; they weren't addicts.

About The Crickets, Joe B. Mauldin did a good stage show and is an excellent stage show man. Also, Buddy was working for a $1000 a week for Alan Freed; Freed really ripped him off. The Summer Dance Party says that it was the Tommy Allsup Western Swing Band, but it was a Blues Band. As I previously stated we had three horns; there wasn't anything western about it. You know, Buddy's career was just a little over a year. He stayed busy during that time. His career was really from September 1957 to February 1959 – about eighteen months.

On the Summer tour when Buddy had his new Lincoln and was driving with The Crickets we were in a station wagon; however, I rode with them some of the time. That's when he kept the money and didn't send it back to Petty. The only time he got to see any of his money was that Summer tour. He told me that he couldn't even write a check, that Petty wrote all the checks. The first check that went into the trust account was for $87,000. That was just the recording contract, not the publishing contract.

Chapter 6
ODESSA and CALIFORNIA and BACK to ODESSA

After the tour in New York City we had two groups of Crickets up there. Those who had done the tour with Buddy and the old Crickets with two new members who had come up with Norman Petty. We met at the GAC office where they said, "Since Tommy helped us finish this tour, we won't book the Crickets unless he's part of the New Crickets". I didn't care one way or the other, but I stayed there with them and we sent Ronnie Smith, Carl Bunch, Sonny Curtis and Waylon Jennings to Texas. Jerry Allison, Joe B. Mauldin, Earl Sinks and I stayed in New York. We stayed there a month, drove down to Baltimore and did a television show, drove to New Jersey and did a show with Xavier Cugat and Abbie Lane where they played a record and you said if it's going to be a hit or not. That's the only thing we did. I told Jerry that I was going back to Texas, that I did not like New York – Buddy Holly is dead, The Crickets are gone – *it's over*. He said that he thought it would break open. I said, "No, get Sonny Curtis to come back and play guitar; I was going back to Odessa and the Silver Saddle, and if Moon is still there with my band I can go back to work". Moon was still there, so I went back with him. Nothing happened for The Crickets; Jerry moved to California, and Joe went to work as an engineer for the studio. And I played a lot of shows with men like Bob Wills.

We stayed there in Odessa until March of 1960, and one morning I went by to get Moon and go eat breakfast. He had said, "Come by, I want to talk to you". So Moon and I went to breakfast, and he said, "Tommy,

I've been talkin' ta Jimmie Davis; he's gonna run for governor, and if you want to go to Louisiana with me and he gets elected we'll have a good job for years". I had heard about this before, back in 1950 when I worked with Preacher Harkness; he said that when Jimmie was elected the first time all they did was sit around with nothing to do and wait for weeks waiting for him to sing. Of course, you get paid for it. I said, "Naw, I think I'm goin' out to California; I've got a job out there that pays real good".

So I moved to California in 1960; Snuff Garrett had signed Bobby Vee, and I started doing rock and roll sessions. Snuff asked if I wanted to be on their session, so I started playing guitar for Bobby Vee and Johnny Burnette. We did an album on The Crickets and put it out on Liberty Records with a new singer named Jerry Naylor. Nothing happened, so Bobby Vee did the "Bobby Vee Salutes The Crickets"; I played all of the guitar solos on it, and The Crickets were a part of it. Still nothing happened. I thought nothing would develop because there was no Buddy Holly; it was just like Bob Wills and Tommy Duncan. When Tommy left Bob he never made it big again. I've never gone out and worked as a Cricket, don't intend to and never intended to. However, they've worked through the years. Buddy was like Hank Williams, he got big after he died. Paul McCartney bought out the catalog and has kept the songs going. He started to play Buddy's songs. I didn't like the movie "The Buddy Holly Story", but Paul produced an excellent documentary, "The Real Buddy Holly Story".

Snuff Garrett was a disc jockey in Wichita Falls when I was playing with Buddy and recording for Petty. He was having a contest in 1958; he had climbed up on a flag pole and wasn't going to come down until so much money was raised for some purpose. Buddy had gone by to see him; they had become pretty good buddies – friends. That's how I met him, through Buddy Holly. What actually took me to California was that I was ready to make a change and had a job with a man named Jack Tucker who was from Ada, Oklahoma. I had worked a little with him in 1955. Jack was building his own club, but when I got there he kept playing his own band. For awhile during the day I pulled car bodies at the General Motors plant. Then I put together a band in Gardena. We played back and forth between Gardena and Long Beach. We were playing a club one night when Snuff walked in with Jerry Allison and said that he was going to be recording Buddy Knox the next Tuesday night – "Do you want to come down and play guitar on it? I need some rock and roll guitar". I said, "Well, I just play what I play". He said, "Well, if you just play what you played with Buddy Holly". I went up there that night, and he had about twenty strings - violins, drums, bass. I went in carrying my Fender amp and Fender Stratocaster – it was the only guitar I had. They said, "Sit up there between those two guitars; Barney Kessel was one guitarist and Howard Roberts was the other. Tommy Tedesco was playing the bass guitar. Here were the best jazz guitarists in the world.

Barney and Howard were on just about every session we did at Liberty; each was great, and it didn't bother me that Barney Kessel was from Muskogee, Oklahoma. We became good friends, and he sold me a good L-5 guitar that I wish I still had. In those days all I had was an old Gibson flat top that I was playing rhythm on.

Ernie Freeman brought music over and said, "Do you read music"? I said, "No". He pointed out places and said that Buddy sings here and here you play. He put "play sixteen bars or eight bars". He said, "Do your solo right here". I thought to myself, "You better not blow this or you won't be back up in these studios". I put in my best lick that I thought I had on it. Ernie afterwards that night said, "You want to start doing some sessions with me"? It seems that the 1960s rock and roll guitars out there were those jazz guitarists. They were great; I didn't really play rock and roll, but what I was doing I guess was closer to what they wanted. So I would go to those sessions, and he would put eight bars or sixteen bars. I probably sneaked into those sessions, but Snuff was responsible for it. About a year later, he said, "Now that you're doing these session, why don't you come down to Liberty Records and I'll get insurance for you and your family, and you'll contract all the sessions". Well, contract was like the leader, you got union double pay.

As stated, there just weren't many rock and roll guitarists in the early '60s. Chuck Berry and me; the early Glenn Campbell and James Burton was just getting started with Ricky Nelson. Burton played a style similar to the Duane Eddy – heavy bass strings stuff. They talked about my licks, but I can't really describe them. I guess my sound was bending the strings with a lot of treble. On the Bobby Vee sessions we had rehearsed "Please Don't Ask About Barbara" in C with open strings; it had been written in C. When we got to the session C was too low; Ernie Freeman said, "We'll move it up to E flat". That blew hell out of my open strings in C. That's when I started thinking about buying a capo. I had to play the same licks that didn't sound as good as they did in open C. I blew about five takes in a row. We were cutting live and had thirteen or fourteen strings. Every time we'd get to the solo, I'd blow it. I finally said, "I can't do it like the demo, because it was in C". If I had had a capo, I could have done it, but even then I didn't really know what a capo was. I didn't own one until I got to Nashville a few years later. It took at least ten takes (some believe that it was fifty-two takes) before we could get it to sound right, but it was a hit.

At Liberty and working with Si Waronker I became the session contractor; they would call and tell me how many musicians they wanted

– maybe eight or ten violins, violas, cellos. At times it was like working with a symphony orchestra. We did sessions with as many as thirty violins, and the Ricky Moreno sessions had fifty musicians.

Session recording worked out alright for a few months, and then Joe Allison who was the country A & R man quit. Joe had produced the Bob Wills and Tommy Duncan album *Together Again*, and at the same time he was working for Liberty he was working for Central Songs. In late 1961 we were at Al Bennett's house, Bennett and Si Waronker were behind Liberty Records; Snuff said that he wanted me to be the Country A & R. Since I had a country background, Snuff put me in charge of the country and western.

Snuff was head of A & R – 21 years old; he was Liberty Records A & R Director. We had been there about a year, and he had already had hits with Bobby Vee, Johnny Burnette and Gene McDaniels. Snuff was hotter than a three dollar pistol. In 1962 Snuff had more hit records that he produced for Liberty than RCA had on their entire label. We were tearing them up. We had Timi Yuro, Gene McDaniels, Johnny Burnette, Bobby Vee – it was all rock – the same stuff I had done with Holly. However, Snuff made a mistake or two. Bobby Vee had been with us in Moorehead, Minnesota and knew a songwriter from around there. Bobby would bring songs to Snuff and say, "I got this weird little cat playing piano for me, and he's writing these off the wall songs". Snuff would say, "I don't have time for that shit". The weird cat became known as Bob Dylan. And when Bobby came back from his European tour, he said, "Snuff, I had a great little backup band in England". Snuff passed on them, too – *they were the Beatles!*

It was nice; I was making some money for a change and was not on the road. I did the Ventures *Twist* album and with Dick Glasser wrote

"Bluer Than Blue" for them. I played on all of Gene McDaniels' records. Johnny Burnette was an early rockabilly star, and I was on every record he cut for Liberty. He stayed in the charts for two or three years with songs like "You're Sixteen" and "Little Boy Blue"; then he was killed in a boating accident. We stayed with Liberty until late '64 or early '65. Snuff wanted to get out, and I had done real well in country/western with Willie Nelson, Bob Wills, Tex Williams, Little Joe Carson, Warren Smith, Gordon Terry and Ray Sanders – those were my acts on Liberty. We were having hit country songs, but country wasn't making money for the label. It was rock and roll that brought in the bucks.

I remember all the big star sessions. I'll start with Willie Nelson; he's the top of my list and had been signed for Liberty by Joe Allison. I met Willie in 1960, and I did my first album with him in '61. I inherited him when I took over the Country A & R at Liberty. Joe had already done an album titled *And Then I Wrote*; they were songs Willie had written. He came out to California; in fact, he moved to California, and we opened an office, a little booking office. There was a lot of talent around Southern California. We sat down and talked. He said, "You know, I've already cut most of my good songs", but he had so many good songs. The first song I cut with him was "Half a Man". He said, "I've got this song that nobody wants to cut". He played it, and it knocked me out, what a beautiful thought the way it is put together. I believed that it was a song that would bust him wide open; so we cut it and sent it out. Disc jockeys started calling Liberty saying, "That song's so morbid we can't play it". I said that it was a beautiful love song; they said that they didn't want to hear about some man having half an arm. I said that everything says "if I had"; there's an "if" in front of all that he says. I said that they were "supposed to be professional and hear what he was saying", but then that's been the story of my life.

Earl Palmer and Leon Russell worked with Willie. The engineer Eddie Bracket who was a great engineer back in those days said, "He has the most cutting voice; you just put the microphone in front of him. You don't have to do anything to him; he has a natural sound coming out of his mouth. He's the star of every recording; you just have to know when he is going to sing". Back then they did the mixing on the date, and he'd hold back. He wasn't breaking time; it was his style. He would catch up at the end of the line. I found out when you played with him in a session, you better make out a chord chart. When he was singing he'd lay back, and he'd be hanging onto a chord when you should have already changed. It was a lot of fun, and I think we made a lot of great records. We cut some more songs; I even tried some western swing like "Roly Poly" and "Right or Wrong". We cut some of his songs that other artists made hits out of in later years. We were cutting the right material, but it just wasn't his time. My first Liberty production was *Here's Willie Nelson* and later did one using everybody's songs except his with strings that came out later on United Artists. He did "Am I Blue" with a beautiful arrangement. Bill Purcel, a great piano player, played some beautiful piano; Bill McAlhaney did the strings arrangement; and the Anita Kerr Singers were on it. It had every ingredient for a hit in it; Cleveland, Ohio stations jumped on it, and two or three big Chicago stations like WLS loved it – but "Bam"!, here came the Beatles. They wiped everything out. We decided to get back to the country stations.

I used Bobby Bruce, the great western swing fiddle player, on quite a few of Willie's early recordings, songs like "Right or Wrong", "Half a Man", "Columbus Stockade Blues" and others. I liked what Jimmy Day was doing with the steel guitar, so for the strings I had Ernie Freeman write out what the steel guitar player had done. Willie was one of the first in country music to use violins; we tried to make the violins play the licks that Jimmy Day played on the steel guitar.

We weren't really trying to go pop; we weren't trying to make a pop artist out of Willie. We were trying to sell records. I tried every conceivable way to promote pop songs and pop tunes; that was in 1962 and '63. Then in 1970 he came out with the *Stardust* album, seven years after what we had done on Liberty and the same kind of material that we had produced. He was getting radio play and disc jockeys loved it, but we couldn't get time in the record stores. The timing was right in 1970, for it stayed on the charts for 300 weeks.

Joe Allison had produced some albums with Bob Wills, so I re-signed Bob for the label. The second album I produced was *Bob Wills Plays and Sings.* You can tell the ones he's playing on because his fiddle is out of tune. Louie Tierney wrote out some parts on them, but Bob wouldn't play them so Louie took over. He had it written out, songs like "Maiden's Prayer" and "Rosetta"; it was great. We had rhythm lines that we used in rock and roll bands. Bob wanted a girl singer and said, "Can you get me one of those who sing real high - I'm talkin' about angels - real high". I said, "Yeh". Vicki Carr was one of my artists at that time. I asked Vicki if she could sing a high falsetto, and she agreed. Then he wanted some background singers; he said, "I've never had background singers". He was thinking "because that's the way country music is moving". I tell people that and they don't believe it, but he told Gene Crownover, "Gene, hit that money pedal". Gene had a steel with pedals, but he still played it the old style. Bob was wanting the commercial sound of the pedal steel.

On one of the songs that Joe Allison put on the *Together Again* album with Tommy Duncan, Bob said, "I got to re-sing a song. Tommy did it so bad, my people out there can't stand it – I'm going' to have to re-do it to get back in good graces with them". Bob and Tommy didn't like one another even though in the early '60s they tried to get along; Bob fired Tommy again. In the spring of 1963 I was putting together a new album, *Bob Wills Sings and Plays*, and Bob and his manager Sam Gibbs asked me to meet them at a dance they were playing at Navasota, Texas – fifty or sixty miles west of Houston. About midnight Bob said, "Tommy, you come and go with me; Luke's gonna bring the band and the bus. We'll drive the car". Sam had been riding with Bob in his big black Pontiac. We left Navasota about midnight and drove to Austin; on the north side we pulled into a motel – the kind with a room and a little garage. Bob said, "Tommy, I believe we're in number 6; we'll see if the door is open". There was no car; no one was there. The door was open, so we went in. There were two beds; we went to sleep. The next morning about seven someone knocked on the door. Bob got up and pulled his pants on. It was the lady who owned the motel. She came in with a big tray of hot biscuits, eggs, bacon, sausage, orange juice and coffee – a complete meal that she set on the table. Bob thanked her and asked her how her husband was. "Fine, he's out of town real sorry he missed you". Bob told her that before we left for San Angelo that he would come up and settle with her. She said, "Oh, no, you won't; my husband would kill me if he thought I charged you for a room". I was telling Luke about it years later, and he said, "I've been all over the country with Bob and people did that. They loved him; there were times when the whole band wasn't allowed to pay". It was an amazing experience for me.

We went to Las Vegas and did a live album with Tex Williams in '63 at the Mint Club, which was pretty neat. Wally Hider who went to San Francisco and became big in rock and roll and developed big studios was

"Old Rivers" session with Walter Brennan; Liberty Records, United Studios in Hollywood, 1963; l to r: Ernie Freeman, arranger; Walter Brennan; Snuff Garrett, producer; Tommy Allsup; Johnny Mann.

working for United Recorders the first couple of years when I was with Snuff Garrett. He was an engineer, and I had seen him around the studio. All of a sudden he had his own studio down the street off of Hollywood Boulevard – just a little over-dub studio where you could go in and put vocals on or add a guitar or re-mix. He was one of the first remote guys; in later years he did all of the big rock groups remote. His first remote job was with me up at the Mint Club Casino in Las Vegas with Tex Williams.

At that time he didn't even have a truck, so we rented a U-Haul truck and put in two three-track machines – that was when we were still recording three-track – and his portable board and mikes. In Vegas he ran the mikes into the lounge on the stage and sat out back recording them. Tex only had about a four or five piece band. He had Billy Armstrong playing fiddle, and I said, "You've got to have two fiddles". Well, Billy Gray was playing across the street at the Golden Nugget, so we borrowed Bobby Creighton, another fiddle player, from Billy. Tex had a guitar player, Chuck Thompson, and I said, "You know, you always had a big band; let's get some more people". So I took Glen Campbell, who was getting started about that time, up with me to play guitar. We got Billy Gray's steel player. I think Tex was only carrying a fiddle, electric guitar, bass and drums. So we ended up with a big band. It turned out to be a pretty good album called *Tex Williams Live in Las Vegas*.

We recorded Walter Brennan doing "Old Rivers" in Hollywood. John Glenn had orbited the earth on February 20, 1962 – the first orbit for the United States. Al Bennett's doctor had written "The Epic Ride of John H.

Tommy's studio band photographed at the Moose Lodge in Odessa, 1965; l to r: Bill Carns, drums; unidentified, bass; Tommy Allsup; Dale Quit, keyboards; Jim Latham, steel guitar.

Glenn" which was a piece of crap. We went into the studio to record it, because Bennett had told us to do it. I had "Old Rivers", so we wound up doing it, too. The rest is history; we had it ready to ship the next day. We went to radio stations and took acetates in, and by morning their phones were burning up – we knew we had a hit. My friend Cliff Crofford wrote it, and I published it. I was the leader in the session. Snuff Garrett was the producer, and Ernie Freeman the arranger; it was 1963 in the Hollywood, United Studios. The interesting thing is that it was a hit with the young people, not the older folks.

Liberty bought Imperial Records and acquired Fats Domino records and Fats as an artist plus Slim Whitman on the country catalog of Imperial. Ricky Nelson was kind of in between. I produced Slim Whitman recordings in about '64. Then Snuff said, "I'm gonna pull away from Liberty and start my own production company, maybe build a studio"; I thought, I want my own studio.

I left Liberty because Snuff left Liberty. By then our country product wasn't selling. The only company selling country back in those days was Decca; they had all of the juke box stuff. Snuff and I decided to start our own studio. I had this big idea about a studio in Odessa with my brother-in-law. At one time Snuff wanted me to move the studio out to California with him, but I didn't want to go back to California. I was there from 1960 to '65 – five years was long enough to live in California. I wanted to get back to Texas, so I left California in 1965 to build a studio in Odessa.

My brother-in-law and I bought some land that had an the alley, and the alley was the city limit. We were just outside the city limits which meant we could build whatever we wanted to. He lived in the next block. We built the studio on one side of the street, and on the other side he had built a fallout shelter – it was when all that scare went on about a nuclear war. I told him that we could take that fallout shelter and make a heck of an echo chamber out of it. We could bury lines across the road and nobody would ever know. The pavement stopped right there at our studio, so we could dig through that. We got a Mexican plaster guy out there and plastered that fallout shelter with epoxy stuff, made it slick as glass and made a wonderful echo chamber.

We put a speaker at one end and had the mikes at one end. We ran the cable under ground because we had to run a cable to the speaker and had to run the cable from the mike back to the studio. We had a good studio. We cut mostly custom sessions and had one hit out of there – "In the Year 2525" with Zager-Evans. We did that in the latter part of '68; it was a big rock and roll hit that came out in early 1969. Denny Zager and Rick Evans were from Lincoln, Nebraska; each played the guitar and sang. They were listed as a folk-rock duo, and their single hit was released as a "regional label" on Truth 8082 [the Odessa label] as "In the Year 2525 (Exordium & Terminus)". It was the number one "Adult Contemporary" hit for two weeks and stayed on the charts for twelve weeks.

We had a label called West Tex and A-OK, and the record broke open in Minneapolis, Minnesota. I had just moved to Nashville in December, 1968 and got a call from my partner in the studio in Odessa; he said that we had an order for 5000 records in Minneapolis. We hadn't sold many of anything, not even fifty of one thing until Zager and Evans busted wide open in Minneapolis. I went down and placed an order with the pressing company in Nashville. It came out in the early part of 1969, and RCA Victor picked it up. They said that it was the biggest record of the year in '69 and sold something like nine million copies worldwide. A lot of things Zager and Evans talked about in that record came true.

Rick Evans and Denny Zager wrote their own stuff; they wrote "In the Year 2525". I think Zager actually wrote it; he sang it for me a few days before we recorded it. Zager came and said they would like to do a session. They played places like the Ramada Inn and other motels singing as a duo; the records were 45rpms and they could take them out and sell them. They could take some of the cost themselves. I said, "Let's do that weird song that you wrote". So we pulled the thing out and recorded it. I took the guitar parts; the horns were two guys who came up from Abilene. You'll hear violins on the records, for six kids in the high school orchestra played them. I mean violins, not fiddles, because they were reading the notes. They were very young, and people would say, "Where'd you get that string section"? They could've been junior high students for all I know.

Bob Wills came to Odessa just before he started touring with Tag Lambert. Jim Blair, Ramona Reed's husband, booked some jobs in the area, and I had a little band we used there in the studio. Bob came out and stayed about a week with us. He wanted to start playing Wednesday, Thursday, Friday, and Saturday evenings in American Legion buildings around West Texas and Oklahoma. He said, "I would like to go play and charge a dollar a person to get in; I think we could draw 500 to 600 maybe 700 people a night. We play these clubs, and they charge $5 or $6 dollars a person. People who like my music can't afford to pay that much to get in". I had this little five piece band – guitar, drums, bass, steel and fiddle and Ramona sang with us. He said, "We'll take your band, and I'll play fiddle; there'll be enough money, and we'll only play four nights a week". Well, we were playing two or three nights out around Odessa, but Bob was serious about it. Jim Blair and I, on different occasions, talked about what might have happened if we had done it.

Bob was wanting to do something; it was after he had lost the band to Carl Johnson or sold the rights and had to front the band with Leon Rausch in it. He had tried using "Bob Wills, the Band with a Beat" as a drawing name because Leon was out working with the Texas Playboys. But, it didn't work. It always seemed wrong that he lost the name, The Texas Playboys; the man didn't give him any money, maybe $10,000. Bob was always in the need for money.

I was in Texas for three years when I got this call from a friend in New York about a job with Metro Media in Nashville. I met the president at the Dallas airport, Love Field. He had said that he wanted to talk to me, and he was going to L. A. He asked how would we recognize each other, and I said that I would have on a cowboy hat. He said that he was a short bald headed Jewish man. We met in the hallway in Love Field. We shook hands, and he went on to Los Angeles. I went back to Odessa and started packing for Nashville – the winter of 1968.

Chapter 7
NASHVILLE and LATER

When I moved to Nashville in December, 1968 the first act I signed with Metro Media was Clay Hart; we had a number one record with him on a song called "Spring". I also signed Chill Wills; Bob Hinkle and I produced and I arranged the selections on *Chill Wills: Hello Cousin*. Working with him was a great experience.

He wanted to eat at Linebaughs; it was next to the Ernest Tubb Record Shop on lower Broadway. Chill Wills told my secretary to call and get us a reservation for lunch; it was a greasy spoon place, and they had never had a reservation request. She called and said that Chill Wills was coming

Chill Wills in Nashville, 1969; l to r: Bob Hinkle, Chill Wills, Tommy Allsup. Photo by Robin Hinkle, Hollywood.

Tommy's mother, Retta Maudine Allsup, Chill Wills, and Tommy, 1969, Nashville. "Bob Hinkle sent of a copy of this picture to my mother; my niece was with her in Claremore when my mother saw the picture. She tore it up. My niece said, 'Grandmaw, why did you tear the picture up?' She said, 'That old flirt kissed me on the cheek and had his arm around me.' She didn't want anyone to see the picture. My sisters had heard about this picture, but had never seen it until recently". Photo by Bob Hinkle, Hollywood.

down and would they set up a big table. We went down to eat, and he said, "I want some of that banana puddin'". They had great banana pudding; it was one of those places where you could walk by and fill up your plate. Chill said, "I want some banana puddin', Cuz". He called everybody "Cousin – Cuz". The woman who ran it said, "I'm sorry, Mr. Wills, but that truck driver over there got the last bowl of pudding". He was sitting at the counter. Chill said, "I've got to have a bite of that banana puddin'; I'm gonna go over there, and maybe he'll give me a bite". He went over and put his arm around the man and said, "Howdy, Cuz, that's mighty fine banana puddin' you've got sittin' there. Ya know, I had my heart set on gettin' some, but they're out of it". The man knew who he was and said,

"Well, take a bite of mine". Chill said, "Well, thank you" and took a bite. He kept on talking , and the man looked at him while he talked and never looked at the pudding. Chill kept talking and eating; he ate that whole bowl of pudding before the man realized what had happened. Chill said, "Cuz, it looks like I ate all your puddin', let me pick up your tab". The man said, "No, that's fine, I'm glad you enjoyed the puddin'". He sat there and talked that man entirely out of his pudding; he ate every bit of it. He was a character; if he was walking down the street and no one was on his side and he saw people on the other side, he would cross over to talk to them and give them a postcard that said, "Hello, Cuz, Chill Wills". He had to have an audience.

In 1969 at the Disc Jockey Convention in Nashville the Metro Media Hospitality Suite was on the sixth floor of the Hermitage. Before it got so big it was at the Andrew Jackson Hotel; you could sit in the mezzanine and watch the d.j.s and the stars. You could walk upstairs and walk down the halls, and there would be jam sessions going on in the rooms. Record labels would have a suite or two; every thing was in one hotel. Then it became so big that they had to add space, and the Hermitage was just a block up the street from the Andrew Jackson.

The Hermitage only had two elevators, and in those days it took a week to get from the first to the sixth floor. Elevators stayed packed; something was happening on every floor. People would ride all the way to the top floor just so they could get off going down. Chill was staying at the Ramada Inn and had taken a laxative. On the way over to the Hermitage he told Bob Hinkle, "We better get on over to the Metro Media Suite; I've got to use the bathroom". They crowded on to the elevator, and Chill was greeting everyone like he always did with "Howdy, Cuz". They got on at the first floor, but every time the elevator started to close someone would stick an arm in the door – it would open and close, open and close. They finally got the door shut and went to the second floor. Bob said that two passengers got out and ten got in. Chill said to Bob, "We better hurry and get to that sixth floor".

Bob said that it took them ten to fifteen minutes to get to the fifth floor where Chill split the people like Moses splitting the Red Sea to get off the elevator. He started knocking on each door as they walked down the hall, but the hospitality suites were on the first and sixth floors. Everything between were private rooms and private parties. He couldn't get anybody to open a door, so he charged for the stairwell. Bob had suggested going behind the curtains at the end of the hall, but he couldn't wait. He threw the door open and said, "Hinkle, hold the door for me". He had to use the bathroom or go in his britches. Bob said that he was squatted down when two couples walked by, and Chill looked at them and asked, "Are you enjoying the convention"? One woman looked at the one she was with and said, "Wasn't that Chill Wills"? The man replied, "I think so". When he got through he used his handkerchief to clean himself and to spread over it so his crap could not be seen. Now he always carried postcards in his inside coat pocket with his picture on it that said, "Howdy, Cousin, Chill Wills", and he would sign his autograph. He stuck one of his cards under his handkerchief and said, "Thank you, Lord".

Bob said that later when they were in the lobby a black man came up with one of Chill's cards and asked for his autograph. Chill asked, "Where did you get that"? The man said, "Some d.j. shit on the stairs and stuck this in it, so I cleaned it off so I could get you to sign it". Chill said, "Give that to me, and I'll give you a clean one".

There was a guitar player, Bucky Meadows, from the '50s with them when they were looking for an open room; he saw me in the hospitality room and was trying to tell me what Chill had done. He was laughing so hard that he could hardly tell the story, and, of course, Chill was over shaking hands with the president of Metro Media and saying "Howdy, Cuz" to everybody. He was just an old man who couldn't wait. In the winter of '69, when Eldon and Ruby Shamblin and the Cummins had the first tribute for Bob Wills in Tulsa, I took Chill to it. He, Roy Acuff, Tex Ritter, Ernest Tubb and I flew together; it was a memorable trip.

I stayed with Metro Media a couple of years, and a man I worked with named Len Levy had been the president of Epic Records started up a label GRT and wanted me to head up it. So I left Metro Media and went with GRT and had Stan Hitchcock, Mac Curtis, Mickey Gilley, Hugh X. Lewis, John Wesley Ryles – it was a good label. We had six songs in the charts when GRT said that they didn't like country music. By then I was so tired of arguing with New York people that I said that I was just going to do sessions. My wife just booked sessions for me at home for several years. That's all I did for about ten years – I mean I hit it hard for years. For ten years I averaged ten sessions a week. From 1970 to 1980 I did 5000 sessions – a ten year period. But, you know many of the men were doing four sessions a day down there.

I got started on *For the Last Time* album in 1973 when Betty Wills called and said that Bob wanted to do one more album, but he had already had a stroke. We talked on the phone and I asked, "Bob, what do you want to record"? He said, "I'd like to get some of the old boys back together; I'm coming to Nashville in October to receive an award from ASCAP". Al and Betty Strickland were going to drive him over. When they arrived in Nashville, Cindy Walker had an apartment in Nashville at that time, and she wanted to see him. I picked her up, and we went over to the motel where they were staying. When we visited with him I said, "Bob, who do you want on the album - Luke"? He said, "No, no, I'm not gonna bring my brothers in; I'd like to have the guys who started with me – Smokey and Al. You know Joe was too pop". Joe Frank had been working pop trios around Fort Worth. He said, "You and Leon [Rausch] can handle bass".

In looking back I've kicked myself many times for not using Herbie [Remington] and [Gene] Crownover as steel players. Merle Haggard heard that Bob was in town and came by the room and said that he would sure like to be on the session. I said, "We'd love to have you on it singing, but we can't afford you, Merle". He said, "I'll work for scale, just like the other guys". Bob asked if I agreed, and I said, "Yeh"! So Merle came in on the album for union scale.

It would have been a really big thing for the Texas Playboys if we hadn't brought Leon McAuliffe in. I had everything set up for national television and bookers, but at that time Leon just didn't want to work. Al and the boys were starving to death, but McAuliffe had made his and didn't want to work. But after the album was released and Bob died and they were hot for awhile with the Johnny Carson Show wanting them and others wanting to book them, then Leon decided to make money off of him.

Of course Cindy Walker wanted to be a part of the sessions; she wrote "Goin' Away Party" which is a classic western swing song on the album along with "What Makes Bob Holler?". She had told me that O. W. Mayo was so nice to her when she was a teenager to get her acquainted with Bob that she said, "Mr. Mayo, I'm going to write you a song and give it to you". She wrote "Blues for Dixie" and gave it to him; she was sincere about it. She said, " I was so happy about Asleep at the Wheel and the award for their version of the song that gave Mr. Mayo recognition before he died". Now, **isn't Cindy Walker great!**

We booked the Sumet-Burnet Studio in Dallas for December 3rd and 4th, 1973 for the recording sessions. We arrived in Fort Worth the day before and had a luncheon at Bob and Betty's home for all of the men participating – Eldon Shamblin, Keith Coleman, Johnny Gimble, Smoky Dacus, Leon Rausch, Hoyle and Jody Nix, Leon McAuliffe, Bob Moore, Al Strickland and Bob and I – Merle Haggard came in on the 4th, and Charles Townsend was with us. Betty fixed the lunch, and we ran over the songs we were planning to record. Bob listened to them and added the songs Cindy Walker had sent to him. He was in a wheelchair at that time.

The next day we went to the Studio and rolled Bob in; he was ready to go and had his white hat on. I had set the band up similar to how he would have set up for dances. I put him in front of Keith, Johnny and Leon with Eldon to the side; he could see Al and Smoky. We cut Cindy's song, "Blue Bonnet Lane". Leon McAuliffe had sung it in a movie, and when we rehearsed it he said, "We ought to kick this off with the steel guitar". Of course Leon wanted to kick every song off with the steel. So we got in the session, and Leon kicked it off and sang it. We played it back, and I pulled a chair up close to Bob and Betty. We were listening to the playback; he was intense, really listening. I said, "The sounds pretty good doesn't it, Bob"? He said, "Let's do it again and let the fiddles kick it off". There wasn't anything McAuliffe could say other than "fine, Bob". Bob was still the leader. We did another take – Bob wanted to hear the fiddles. After that most of what we recorded that day we kicked off with the fiddles. That's what he liked and that's what he wanted. Bob had his input in that session.

He got mad at himself, because when we were recording "What Makes Bob Holler"?, he was trying to talk his lines – *he just couldn't get them*. It was sad. Finally, he said, "Let Hoyle do my talkin'". Hoyle wasn't familiar with the song and had difficulty, but he got through it. Betty said that night Bob was really disgusted with himself because he couldn't participate more in the session. We had picked out the songs – Bob and I. He did much in making the sessions successful, but he was really mad because he couldn't do "What Makes Bob Holler"?. That was the proverbial straw that broke the camel's back. That night he had the big stroke.

Bob did get to hear the album. As soon as I got it back to Nashville and mixed it down, I sent Betty a tape. She played it for him a number of times and said that he really liked it. He had some of the men together who had started with him in Tulsa. I think he went out on a happy note. He was on the last record with some of the guys who were with him on his first Playboy record. I wish we could have included Johnnie Lee and some of the others.

Haggard got there the next day; he didn't get to see Bob in the studio. We had missed singing the theme song, waiting for Haggard to sing it. We went back to the Studio and one thing led to another. He sang "Yearning" and something else. The United Artists men said, "Tommy, we have fifteen songs; why don't you do five or six more, and we might make a double album out of it". So we did enough for a double album. I was an independent producer and had a contract with United Artists for that project. I made all of the arrangements, and they agreed to underwrite the costs.

The first session was pretty emotional; many of Bob's old buddies and their relatives were there. One of Elvis Presley's close friends, Lamar Fike, was there. I said, "Lamar, I didn't know you liked Bob Wills". He said, "Yeh, I love it". When they wheeled Bob in most of them had not seen him in a wheelchair. There weren't many dry eyes. McAuliffe said,

"I think we should go ahead and do "San Antonio Rose" and holler since Bob wants to do "What Makes Bob Holler?"".

The next morning we learned that he had a bad stroke. Before the session started Betty called me and said, "I've got bad news; we can't come over today because Bob had a bad stroke during the night. We can't move him". I didn't say anything. Al Strickland knew because he had gone by to pick them up. Then we told the other guys. It shook everybody up, especially Merle Haggard; he had wanted to be there with Bob. But Bob was there in spirit; he died May 13, 1975.

When we did the *For the Last Time* album I got Bob a big advance up front. I got him $10,000 per album, and we did a double album. Charles Townsend got a Grammy for his liner notes, and I was awarded the Wrangler by the National Cowboy Hall of Fame for the best western album of the year. Then I put together the *Live in Concert* album, some of the old radio shows – I got Betty $25,000 up front for that. Bob probably had the greatest impact on a form of music than anyone – the songs that he had out as well as the ones he inspired. In Bob's mind he wasn't famous, but I get letters from all over wanting Bob Wills albums. He had more product out than most entertainers, and it is amazing the number of good songs that he recorded.

After the attention For the Last Time received, I got a contract for the Texas Playboys with Capitol Records. We were going to call the album *The Original Texas Playboys*. It was a way where I could get Betty some front money; I got her a contract. Leon McAuliffe was to be the leader of the band. That's where I screwed up. He took over and after Johnny Gimble and I quit, it became more of a Cimarron Boys than a Texas Playboys band. I didn't like that, and I told Leon. We had recorded an album in Dallas, and then went to Knott's Berry Farm to record a live album with Asleep at the Wheel and the Texas Playboys. Leon kept bringing in different men. I said, "Leon, I don't want a Cimarron Boys band; I want a Texas Playboys band and sound". He had already started changing things. He was just supposed to front the band, not take it over. He got mad at me, and the next thing I know I got a call from my friend at Capitol who said that McAuliffe wanted to do another album in Hollywood with a different producer. I said, "I've known Leon a long time, and that doesn't surprise me one bit".

They went to Hollywood, and they recorded and they recorded and they recorded – several days of recording, and nothing came of it. They didn't have one thing they could release. The new producer said that maybe they should go to Texas where *For the Last Time* was cut. So they go to Texas and recorded and recorded and recorded and still couldn't come up with the sound the producer was looking for. The reason was that he was looking for the Bob Wills sound but was getting the Leon McAuliffe sound. Leon had some good musicians from his Cimarron days – Bob Kizer, Rudy Martin, Gene Gasaway, Smoky Dacus, Jack Stidham, along with Al Strickland, Joe Ferguson, Bob Boatright and Leon Rausch. It just didn't jell, so Capitol dropped them.

Leon called me and said, "Capitol is about to drop us; do you think you could fix the albums we recorded"? I said, "I don't want anything to do with them". I wasn't mad; he did what he wanted to do. To me, it's a business; I do what I like to do, or I wouldn't be there.

Then they signed with that small Texas label, Delta Records, and they put out some stuff that I think would have made Bob roll over in his grave if he heard it. They got some bad reviews on some of the albums; it didn't even sound like Bob Wills and the Texas Playboys. I was half way mad at some of the men for going along with him. I know that if I had been in the band I would have said, "I'm not goin' ta record that crap". Eldon Shamblin needed the money, so I can't criticize him. He said that when Leon called him to join the group, he said, "Leon, I don't like you and never did; if I don't have to associate with you before or after a show I'll join the group". Leon agreed to it, because he needed Eldon. Johnnie Lee didn't like to see him making money off of his brother's name, so he refused to join them and to go to any tribute where they played.

I worked with Bob, and I produced Bob albums. I talked with him a lot, and I knew what Bob liked. I knew what made him smile, and I know that the albums they were putting out were not making any money. I don't know why Delta was doing it. Anyhow, I had the pleasure of saying "No, Thanks" when he called and asked for help. Right is right, and wrong is wrong; he did me wrong, and that's the way it was. I should have used Herbie Remington or Gene Crownover on *For the Last Time* and none of that would have happened. The Johnnie Lee Wills Reunion album that Steve Ripley produced is a good album; they knew what made Bob, Johnnie Lee and western swing holler.

In due respect for Leon, his Cimarron Boys band was as good as any band assembled, and he had his sound. He had Cecil Brower, Keith Coleman, Ted Adams and other great western swing musicians, and he had his sound. It was his sound. He put the clarinet lead on top of the melody line with his fiddles – like an orchestra, the clarinet lead is on top. The clarinet works well with fiddles. When you listen to Gene Autry music, the clarinet is below the fiddles.

Spade Cooley always had three fiddles. They would play in unison above the lead line. Buddy Spicher was listening to Cooley, and said, "There aren't three fiddlers in Nashville who can play unison in tune like that". And there are great fiddle players in Nashville. Cooley had many of his harmonies above the lead line. Leon also used his fiddles like a tailgate trombone in a Dixieland band. Bob voiced his fiddles one above and one below the lead line. He usually led with the second part below and the third part above, the same way you do guitars. Now four part harmony has to be written out; you usually can't do it in your head or by ear unless you memorize it. When you do parallel harmony, one part above and one part below, sometimes you have to switch – the second part above and the third part below. You can't say that you're going to play the third above and keep it that way. At some point the two outside parts are going to have to swap. A good example is the Sons of the Pioneers harmony; one man may be harmonizing high when the lead jumps and the harmony goes below.

The Bob Wills sound was to get the rhythm right – guitar, bass, drums and piano. These instruments are made to blend with each other if played and produced right. When we had a stand up bass we kept the drum down where you could hear the bass. Today with amps it's all the same audio level. When I started we played to two thousand people with amps and sound that wouldn't even cover a small room today. We played with speakers on the wall, and Bob would say, "They'll come up and hear us; we'll make them come to us; we won't play to that guy standing in the back a hundred yards away; we're not gonna blow the heads off of these people close to the stage". That's why people gathered around the stage when Bob played; they could hear the music and see the show. People at the back could dance; they could hear enough to dance. When it came to piano players, Bob had better ones than Kelso, but none could play better rhythm. Kelso could stomp that rhythm.

There were times when Johnnie Lee Wills had a better rhythm section than Bob, and times when Bob was better. Even if they didn't have a great rhythm section each still had a great dance beat. It was the way they played their tunes. You noticed Johnnie Lee's rhythm section more because he didn't have his fiddles amplified. They played into the mike and played a lot softer than Bob. Bob and his fiddlers really cranked it up. The fiddles were loud, and you didn't hear the rhythm section as much. Also, when Bob didn't have Eldon Shamblin I didn't like his sound that much. The records with Eldon in the band just have a better sound. Eldon was the driving rhythm force; part of the Bob Wills sound was hearing those guitar runs. They used to say to me, "Tommy, play some of those Eldon runs".

Before Eldon joined Bob, they had that old hen house rhythm. That's the only thing I had against Milton Brown's recordings – some of that old western swing wasn't western swing. Some of the older guys around Fort Worth would want to chop my head off when I told them that. It was chicken pickin' hen house rhythm; that's what it sounded like.

I had a studio in Nashville in the early '90s. My engineer Lew Bradley and I had a bunch of old Bob Wills tapes. Lew would go through them to hear Bob tell Tommy Duncan to sing "I Ain't Got Nobody". Bob said that anyone who could sing it like Emmett Miller could go to work for him; it's a tape of the session they cut in Dallas in '36. It was Johnnie Lee on banjo, Herman Arnspiger and Sleepy Johnson on rhythm guitars, Son Lansford on bass, Al Strickland may have been on piano and Bob playing fiddle. We put a click track on it one time, and it didn't vary. I think it was Johnnie Lee's banjo that held it together. Song writers and singers would come into the studio to cut demos, and Lew would play that song for them. He would say, "I want you to listen to this rhythm". A click track is an electric drummer. Lew would show that the rhythm didn't move at all during that three minute record. A good drummer can hold you, but usually you'll rush it a little. When you set that click track it does not move, and when that record ended the rhythm was right there. It was Johnnie Lee; he played rhythm guitar behind his daddy, Uncle John Wills, for years. Uncle John was a great old time fiddler.

After the strong rhythm, Bob's sound was the fiddles. You have to have fiddles and a steel player who knows how to play the chimes behind the fiddles. His front line was fiddles, steel guitar, horns and electric guitar. In today's bands you'll see the fiddles behind the front line. That aggravates the hell out of me; I want the fiddles up front. The instruments supposed to be at the back are the drums and bass.

The first time I *really* worked with Bob was on the first album I produced, *Bob Wills Sings and Plays*. I played guitar on it and then I went back to Odessa and played some jobs with him. When I was with Johnnie Lee, I worked a few shows with him, but it was record production when I really work with him. I mentioned another album that I produced, Bob Wills Live in Concert; this was a time consuming, hard, difficult project.

Bill Mack, the popular Dallas disc jockey and song writer, had given Betty some tapes of radio shows that Bob had made. I had 7 1/2" reel to reel tapes that had been mono recorded in the radio station. The station made copies and gave them to Bill Mack. I had to listen to six months of radio broadcasts to get enough material to put an album together. I might have four different cuts of one person singing a song. I'd have to take the intro off of one cut and mix it with a part off of another cut. It was a nightmare, because everything was mono – not like a multi-track tape. It was difficult; I had to put a little bit here with a little bit there. I had to get Bill and Bob talking and then get the right intro of a song. I then took the music and stripped the bottom out of it; the bass players were playing out of tune. In those days they were notorious at telling Joe Andrews the wrong changes. The drums were good; Crownover's steel guitar was good; the fiddles and talking were good; and Bob's breakdowns were good. I had to overdub most of the rhythm guitar and bass as well as a little snare drum. I brought Al Strickland in to dub over some piano. There had been some piano breaks, but apparently he had no amp – you couldn't hear it. I had Al play the breaks. It took a lot of work to put it together.

There is an eight minute version of "St. Louis Blues" that I had recorded with Bob out in California in '63. I called and they sent me a tape. United Artists had purchased Liberty, and Capitol had purchased United Artists, so they had it in their vault. The musicians were almost the same as the radio show. A lot goes on in the studios that people don't know about. We have machines that can tune people up who sing flat. You hear singers who sound great on record, but when you hear them live, they don't sound so good. We tune them up in the studio, and I can tune up a fiddle or guitar that's flat or sharp. I had to re-work a bass solo on one of my instrumental albums, and the bass player who shall remain anonymous later said, "I played better bass than I thought I did". I never told him what I had done.

I've worked with many stars and so called stars, but the two who effected me in my lifetime were charismatic men – Bob Wills and Elvis Presley. Bob had as much as Elvis, but he had something more that would draw people to him. It was his fiddle playing – *the way he played his fiddle.* Johnnie Lee was an excellent band leader, but not a salesman like Bob. Bob could sell a band. Johnnie Lee could take a good band and make it sound good, but Bob could take a band that wasn't good and make it sound good. I've seen him walk on stage, and it sounded as if each band member had been pulled off and replaced by a better musician.

114

I first met Elvis in '61 or '62 when I was doing a rock and roll album with Johnny Burnette. Elvis was living up in the Hollywood Hills before he started entertaining in Vegas. We finished the session that night, and Johnny, his brother Dorsey and I left the United Studios to go down the street to have a beer. Johnny said, "Elvis is having a party tonight, and we can go – but let's have a drink before we go, 'cause when we get there it'll be nothin' but Cokes". Johnny was correct; when we got there Elvis had a bar set up, but they were serving nothing but Cokes and Seven-Up. People were sitting around the room, and when Elvis walked in he lit the room up. I thought maybe it was just because I wanted to meet him so bad, but later I saw him perform in Vegas. Snuff Garrett and I went to see him, and I realized that he really had charisma.

I did sixty-five demos for a song writer from New York, Ben Wiseman. He came to California in the early '60s to do the demos. Elvis recorded some of them. When his records were released I would hear my guitar licks that I had put on the demos, but I never was in an Elvis session. I did get to work with Dolly Parton, so that made up for missing Elvis.

If someone says that he saw Bob in Vegas and Bob didn't have charisma, he may be right because Bob *did not* like playing in Vegas. If you saw Bob play at Cain's Ballroom in Tulsa, or the Trianon in Oklahoma City, or the American Legion Hall in Seminole or McAlester you saw the real charismatic Bob Wills. If anyone saw Bob riding down the street on his horse leading a parade like Johnnie Lee often did, he understands the real Bob Wills – not the Vegas Bob.

Ray Benson came to Nashville wanting to make an album; he had made a demo for Jim Fogelsong at Dot Records, and Buddy Spicher had played fiddle on the demo. Ray asked if there was any western swing in Nashville. Buddy said, "Yeh, if you want to do an album, you should get Tommy Allsup to produce it". Ray called me just before Fan Fair; this was when Fan Fair was at the Municipal Auditorium. I told him that I would be at the CBS show playing in the band; we agreed to meet, and he said that he would be the tallest one with a cowboy hat. It was June 1972, and we started talking about what to do. He told me that United Artists had agreed to put out an album, and he wanted to cut it that fall. I rehearsed them for about a month for that first album called *Comin' Right at Ya*. I had a production agreement with United Artists that after the production money was recouped, I would get royalties. I didn't know United Artists had agreed to buy them a bus. They bought them an old Greyhound bus; about three years ago the album broke out of the red. Capitol owns it now. Today the music videos are eating the artists' royalties alive; the companies don't care what it costs, because they hold it out of the artist's royalties. You have to sell a lot of product just to break even.

I did the "Route 66" arrangement for them that became so popular; it was a heavy left hand on the piano and the bass. That was the version that hit the charts; the album was *Wheelin' and Dealin'* on Capitol. However, their biggest hit was a country song that I produced for them "The Letter That Johnny Walker Read".

In looking back, I went to Nashville in '62 to record and do sessions with Willie Nelson, and then we recorded Gordon Terry in Nashville. I also did my first Joe Carson sessions in Nashville. So in the three years I was with Liberty, I had become acquainted with many people in Nashville. When I moved there in '68, they had kinda accepted me as one of them, but life there had become hectic.

When I left there in 1979 to go to Texas to get in the club business,

116

we were doing so many sessions that it wasn't fun. The men would be fussing about stuff that wasn't anything. My wife was ready to start singing again, so I said let's go down to Texas and have our own night club and our own band. We went to Fort Worth and took about a year to find a good location. Our partner Herb Graham and I put this club together. I wanted live music, but he was into disco music. So we came to an agreement, we had thirty minutes of live music followed by thirty minutes of recorded music. We had solid music all night long; it lasted six years in Fort Worth as the New West Club. We had built a cover over a court yard, and opened in November 1980 and closed in January 1987.

The neighbors fought us for six years. We were so popular and had such large crowds that people were parking blocks around in the neighborhood. In mid-'80s when the oil prices went down business started falling off. We saw that it wasn't going to come back, and the new owners of the shopping center wanted it back. We had a ten year lease, but we knew we couldn't continue. That's when we went to Dallas and opened Tommy's Heads Up Saloon which lasted about four months. We opened it in October, and it may have been successful if that Blue Monday had not have happened in October of 1987. They had about ten million dollars dedicated to renovating or restoring a block down on "Deep Elum" (traditional pronunciation for Elm). The first thing that opened was the Tommy's Heads Up Saloon; if the others who should have opened up had it would have been good. They didn't. And we bellied up. There were to be four night clubs and a brewery, a couple of restaurants, a park for outside concerts – but it failed. What I regret is stopping in Dallas; I should have gone on back to Nashville. When it went under I decided that we had had some good years in the club business, but insurance got so high, drinking laws got so strict that I decided to go back to Tennessee and record.

I did a few session while we were in Texas, but when we left Nashville in '79 there were men who were playing but were physically, emotionally and musically burned out. I don't know how they stayed in there day after day, but when I got back to Nashville my brain was working again. I could go in the studio and think again. It did me good to get away from it for eight years. I'm doing a lot of gospel session work now, and I did a gospel album. We did basically what we did on country albums; I use the same guys – the older guys who aren't getting much work with the new artists. I like gospel. It's where some of the newer artists are getting started.

The country stars are high priced and it takes so much money to get a record out. The record management will say that it takes a half million to make it big in country music, but I don't agree with that. They say that it takes $150,000 to cut an album – that's silly. Some studio owners do charge that because the money is going straight into their pocket. It's the artist who is getting cheated. It isn't the label, because they get their money. The artists are paying for it, and the producer is getting his money. That's why they go in and spend a month in the studio. I didn't grow up in that school, and I don't believe in it.

It's hard to get any station to play an independent label. The play list is down to forty songs, and they won't even play the older artists. But there has to be a change in radio. I haven't been into promotion, but after Leon Rausch and I did the Wills boxed set I did some promotion. I have a friend in Tallahassee, Florida with a station that plays all requests with a little new stuff. They are the number one station in their area. The sad thing that is happening is that most station owners and managers believe that no one wants to hear Bob Wills and other music legends in drive time, so they only play top forty. When you travel the country you hear the same thing – no variety. Radio is hurting. You know, there are old people who drive to work; the drivers aren't just young folks. You can't do payola with the disc jockeys any more, because you have to deal with the program managers or music directors. I imagine the opportunity to deal with them is there, but the d. j's. don't make the play list.

There are some good singers in the new acts, but there are no great singers. There are no Merle Haggards, Lefty Frizzels. As far as I'm concerned, George Strait is the last original singer to make big; the others copy styles. George Strait and LeAnn Rimes are the last two originals in recent years. The sad thing is that now days the stations force people to listen to some average singers, and soon the people believe that they are great.

Western swing is dance music. Dances were Bob, Johnnie Lee, Leon, Hank, mine and other western swing artists' living. Bill Boyd and bands like that weren't dance bands; they were stage bands and weren't western swing. They may have been western, but not swing. I've offended people by saying that Spade Cooley was the Lawrence Welk of western swing. No offense intended for both bands were good, but Lawrence Welk was no Tommy Dorsey. And Spade Cooley was no Bob Wills. Spade Cooley played Cain's during the rodeo when I was young, and there weren't 300 people there. Archie Bingham and I were going to see him, but Spade had been at the rodeo and was late getting there. Jimmy Widener was fronting the band when they started. Spade had good guitars: Jimmy Wyble, Cameron Hill and Noel Boggs; the rest was pretty much a horn band. Tex Williams told me that Spade never could work back in this country very well; he couldn't draw. Oklahoma and Texas dancers did not go to Cooley's dances. Cooley didn't have the Wills sound; Leon McAuliffe had a little of the Wills sound through the years, but he was only popular in the southwest. I saw Leon in Los Angeles in 1960 at the Foothill Club,

119

and there weren't thirty people there. They just didn't know who Leon was; they knew "Take It Away Leon" but didn't identify it with him. Of course, Bob had charisma and drew large crowds.

Tommy Duncan came to Tulsa back when I was young; he had Jimmy Wyble, Cameron Hill, Noel Boggs, David Coleman, Millard Kelso, Glynn Duncan and Joe Holly and Ocie Stockard on fiddles. They were the "All Stars", but they sounded like the Oklahoma Swing Billies. I was really disappointed. They were sitting there playing for the money, not for the love and fun of it. Tommy Duncan just couldn't get a good sound out of them; like Milton Brown, Tommy was a singer, not a musician – the band led him. I had seen those men play for Bob and Spade; they were great musicians without leadership. If you're going to be a big leader, you have to know people's limitations, know your band members and know what they can do best and let them do what they do best. You don't try to make them do more than they're capable of doing. If you do, they'll screw up; I learned that in studio work. A band requires leadership.

I could put a band together and play nothing but Hank Williams songs and make it western swing. It's the way you play the songs. When you get out of that 2/4 mentality rhythm, change the rhythm and put some hot licks in it you have western swing. That may not sound like the old Wills' musicians, but Bob played everything. He played Eddie Arnold songs, whatever was popular on the radio; it didn't have to be a song written by Cindy Walker or other western swing writers. And everything that happens in western swing is accidental; you can't plan anything. You can have a direction, but when Bob gave Junior Barnard a chorus he had no idea how it was going to turn out. He knew it would be good, but he didn't know what it was going to be. When he gave a man a solo, he didn't know what they were going to play – and they didn't either. Stringed instruments are the foundation of western swing, so no matter what has been written and told about how and why Bob Wills used horns in Tulsa, his primary purpose was to help override the hillbilly music image with the musicians union.

Back in 1969 when I moved to Nashville, there were some boys who had a bluegrass band, the McCormick Brothers, and I wanted to put out an album titled "Brass Meets Grass". I got an arranger, Curley Chalker on steel, Buddy Harmon on drums, Henry Strzelecki on up-right bass and we went in to the studio and did some bluegrass songs with the McCormick Brothers. Curley and Buddy might do something with swing, and then we would resolve it into a bluegrass feel. We had some brass come in. We did "Bad Moon Rising" with the bluegrass guy kicking it off on banjo, and then the brass came in. We really had them swinging in the 4/4 rhythm. My arranger, Bill Walker, said that he wanted to take it over and play it for Chet Atkins and the men at RCA. Before I could get my album out here came Danny Davis and the Nashville Brass with "Wabash Cannonball". To this day I still believe they heard what I had done. I had called Bill Mack, and he mentioned it on the radio. It was one of my first projects in Nashville, probably January or February, 1969. I was so damn mad when I heard Danny Davis because he had been an A & R man at RCA. This happens all the time.

The McCormick Brothers had been on Columbia back in the '50s and had a hit called "The Little Red Rooster Boogie" or something like that. They had a couple of kids playing the trumpet and went to some of these bluegrass festivals, and they nearly ran them out of those bluegrass parks back in Virginia and places like that. They said that the horns weren't too well appreciated, but I thought that it was a good concept of music. But Danny Davis and the Nashville Brass hit so big that my concept was dead.

The record "Spring" by Clay Hart that I produced was nominated for a Grammy. The "In the Year 2525" was nominated for a lot of things, but it was a rock and roll record. Then "For the Last Time" album and some of the early Asleep At the Wheel songs that I produced were nominated for awards. I produced the first five albums that they did, and they won several awards. I did an instrumental "The Hits of Charley Pride" in 1969 that was nominated for a Grammy.

Walter Brennan's "Old Rivers" won just about everything; Snuff Garrett was the producer. I found the song, talked them in to doing it. Right afterwards we did "Old Rivers"; I was the publisher and Cliff Crofford wrote it, and the Lettermen recorded it on Capitol. It was a take off or funny version; instead of "plowed ground" they said "ground round". Brennan came down to Liberty one day and threw that record on Snuff Garrett's desk and said, "Play this damn thing; listen to this"! Snuff played it, and Brennan asked what could be done about it. We already had the number one play around the world. Snuff said that we couldn't do anything, because they didn't take any writer credit for it; plus, we didn't tell Brennan, but the director of my publishing company had given them permission to do it. Actually, I didn't know about it until it came out. Dick Glasser was in charge of Liberty Publishing and he was taking care of my company. When Snuff said that there was nothing we could do about it, Brennan said, "Yes, there is; we can go over to that tower and kick their ass all over the place".

He was ready to go get them; he was a super person. You never saw him when he didn't have a suit and tie on; he was the complete opposite of his role, Grandpa McCoy. We did three albums with him, and Cliff Crofford and I had about twenty of his songs. We wrote and published them, and we worked with him a lot, teaching and recording the songs.

122

We might be walking down the street to the restaurant near the studio, and you couldn't walk fifty feet before someone would roll down their car window and yell, "Hey, Grandpa". When they said, "Grandpa", he would go into that walk identified with the role he played. It was automatic; he transformed himself immediately. If someone said something to him in the restaurant about Grandpa, he would go into that talk. I guess that's why he was a great actor. He said that he had to put a tack in his shoe to limp like that when he first started the role. He didn't want to be caught not limping; that tack always made him limp.

Walter Brennan and Chill Wills were not musicians, and I did an album in 1967 or '68 with "Doc" on *Gunsmoke*. When I had the studio in Odessa he and Festus (Ken Curtis) came in for the rodeo with the Frontiersmen. I knew the Frontiersmen, and they came in one day and said that Doc (Milburn Stone) wanted to record a song. I said, "Great"! So they came over, and you know Festus was a great singer and had been with the Sons of the Pioneers; Doc had some excellent songs and poems he had written. We went ahead and recorded enough for an album, and I leased it to Mercury Records but it never came out. I went out to Hollywood and the Gunsmoke set, and Doc showed me around. He was a great narrator. He told this poem about a man's three best friends – a good horse, a good dog and a good woman. He had some excellent material. We played some melodies behind his narrations, and Festus would sing along. He had a poem about Maggie, and Ken sang the song, "I wander today through the hills Maggie". It was beautiful, and it was part of their rodeo act.

They had an agent on the Coast who would call and have me back up a few acts like theirs. I played for Robert Conrad when he had the television show, *The Wild West*. We were sitting out in the middle of the arena at Odessa, and he was supposed to ride out on his horse and have a fight with this bad man. He was going to tackle this guy, but the first thing he did was break either his ankle or wrist – the very first night, the very first bat out of the bag. They had all of these props shipped in; these chairs that weighted a half pound that they would break over their heads. They were all out in the arena, but his broken bone blew hell out of that performance. He dived off of that horse, and of course, they blamed the horse – it turned the wrong way or something.

I did some recitations with Ralph Emery back in the '60s. We did "The Touch of the Master's Hand" that Tex Ritter had done a few years before. Tex had an organ in the background with sustained chords, but I put an actual melody to it. With Ralph it was a pretty good record; to this day he says that it was one of the favorite things he recorded. We cut it in Nashville with the band, and then I took it to California and put Bobby Bruce on with his violin playing the fiddle part. It wasn't a monstrous record, but it received good air play.

I did a lot of rock and roll in the early '60s; I enjoyed it, but it was strictly to make money. I didn't mind Buddy Holly because I was young and it was new music. He was such a neat person, and I liked his songs. Most rock and roll I didn't really care for; however, most of it was pretty good until the late '60s when they went crazy with it. The late '50s and early '60s rock and roll still had a melody that you could sing to. Buddy had a lot of stage appeal; he didn't have the charisma that Elvis and Bob Wills had, but he certainly had stage appeal. And he had some powerful songs. In a very short time people knew who he was. People knew who he was when he walked into a room because of those big black glasses. Bob Wills didn't realize how popular he was; I believe that he died not knowing how popular and how much he had contributed to musical America.

124

I'm proud of a lot of the records I cut with artists like Charlie Rich, Tammy Wynette, George Jones and others. I'm really proud of the *For the Last Time* album. I can die proud of my life in music. I'm proud of the Joe Carson recordings. He was from Texas and came to work for me in Lawton when he was sixteen years old. Hank Thompson took him to Nashville later that year and he recorded for Mercury, but it didn't sell. So in the summer of 1956, Hank took him to California and Capitol Records where we did a session with him. Nothing happened with those. When I went with Liberty, even though they already had a country roster, he was one of the first I signed. He had a successful record, "I've Got to Get Drunk". His biggest record was "Helpless". About a year after our sessions he was in Wichita Falls, Texas to see his new baby, and pulled out into the by-pass and hit the abutment. It threw him out and killed him. A seat belt would have saved him; it was a freak accident.

In December, 1997 Leon Rausch and I recorded *A Tribute to the Music of Bob Wills*. It's a collection of seven decades of music – fifty numbers on three compact discs or cassettes. Russell Sims of Sims Records produced it, and we called in some of the best western swing musicians: Tommy Morrell, steel guitar; Rich O'Brien, guitar and fiddle; Snuffy Elmore, fiddle; Bob Boatright, fiddle; Buddy Spicher, fiddle; Curley Hollingsworth, piano; Tommy Thatcher, drums; Mark Abbott, upright bass; Dave Alexander, trumpet; Glen Rothstein, sax and clarinet; Tumbleweed Tex, trombone, and I played guitar and banjo and sang a little harmony behind Leon who did the vocals. A couple of years later I worked with Russell Sims in recording Waitin' for a Train, one hundred and nine Jimmie Rodgers songs sung by Dean Mitchell; I played guitar on those Rodgers songs.

In 1997 I produced along with Lanny Fiel and Frankie McWhorter

The Ranch Dance Fiddle: Frankie McWhorter for Fiel Publications in Lubbock, Texas. We recorded and mixed it in Lanny Fiel's studio. Of course it features the cowboy fiddler, Frankie McWhorter, who used to work with Bob Wills, and we brought in Curley Hollingsworth on the piano, Jim Benjamin on drums, the veteran swing steel guitar man, Bobby Koefer, Tommy Morrell on the dobro, Frankie's son Larry McWhorter on the clarinet, Lanny Fiel played mandolin and standard guitar, Leon Rausch sang a few vocals and I played bass, electric guitar and acoustic guitar. It is an excellent collection of old time ranch house fiddle tunes played by a "real working cowboy". We followed that with another Frankie McWhorter collection in 1999, *Texas Sandman.*

Chapter 8
MORE SESSION MEMORIES

Kenny Rogers came into Nashville; Larry Butler picked him up for United Artists Records and signed him. We did some early stuff with him; he'd had a couple of big pop records and was a little bit reluctant to cut country, but after he cut "Lucille" which made a monster hit he was glad to come in and cut some like "The Gambler". He liked his records really polished, and he was fairly easy to record with. He was a good singer – a good artist, easy to work with. He kinda argued with Larry Butler a little bit about the "Coward of the County", but you know A. & R. guys have to twist their arms a bit. I was on sessions or leader of the sessions; I was doing session work in Nashville. I went up to Nashville to run a record label back in December '68. After a couple of years, I got so busy playing sessions that I lost all interest in running a label. I was really getting into the swing of Nashville. I had known the guys there 'cause I use to go there with Willie in the '60s – recorded Willie Nelson, Joe Carson, Tex Williams, Warren Smith – we cut a lot of their stuff in Nashville. I already knew musicians that I liked. They started calling me for session work, and it's pretty demanding. You might have a 10-2-6 session. You work from 10:00 to 1:00, break for lunch, go to the next session that might be at a studio twenty miles away, work from 2:00 'til 5:00. Then you break from 5:00 to 6:00 for dinner, then at 6:00 another session maybe at another studio. If you're lucky, they're at the same place. Sometimes you might play four different sessions at four different studios.

There was Bradley's Barn – Owen Bradley. When he built the first studio he sold it to Columbia, and in his contract he couldn't have another studio in that county. So he just went right over the county line and built one near Hickory Lake – the Barn. It was about a twenty-five to thirty mile drive out there from Nashville, so if you were working in town it was a quick drive. They tried to do a lot of night sessions so the guys could end up out there near the Lake. It was always fun to be out there – it got you out of town. It was way out of town – nowhere, but you better not be behind me 'cause I might stop and get something along the way. It was a two lane road.

I think the '70s were the best years. I look back and think I was really fortunate to be in Nashville during all of the '70s. I was gone a little bit during the '80s and then back in the '90s. It really changed; the whole scene changed from the '70s to the '90s. I think those were the golden years for great country entertainers like Charlie Rich, Kenny Rogers, George Jones, Tammy Wynette, Johnny Paycheck, Johnny Rodriguez. I was just really lucky to get to play on a lot of those sessions – the 1970s. In the '80s new artists started coming in, and the sounds started changing a lot. It's a little more rock than when I was with Buddy Holly.

I was really glad cutting with George Jones; "The Grand Tour" was the first I cut with him, and I worked with him all through the '70s. I recorded all of the George and Tammy Wynette duet sessions. Tammy was a pleasure to record with; she was so professional. She would walk in – he would walk in – both of them had such great voices, and they could get the song in one take. We'd run the song down and maybe make up instrument changes. The voices might change some. The next take you had to be on your toes, because they were going to nail it. Those were the days before punching in your part. They would just get back and sing;

they were really fun. Their duets were great.

I was there when "Behind Closed Doors" was cut with Charlie Rich. Kenny O'Dell, a good friend of mine, had written the song; so the night we cut "Behind Closed Doors" Kenny was out in the parking lot, and when we came out Kenny said, "Did he get to my song today"? I said, "Yeh, he got to it. Man, you've got a hit". You could just feel it; you can feel a hit sometimes. We tried that song with two or three different rhythms; we tried blues and rock, so finally, Billy said, "Let's just cut it country, Charlie". To Pig Robbins, a blind piano player and probably the best in the world and who has been on more records than anybody and has probably been on twenty thousand sessions, Charlie said, "Pig work me up a little intro on that". Right off the top of his head Pig got the little lick that opens it. We cut the song with one more take, and that was it. We had worked on it for two hours trying to get a groove on it. That's what they call magic in the studio; those days are about over.

I got Tex Williams for Liberty. I'd always been a big fan of Tex Williams. He had just shut down Riverside Rancho and had built him a place up in the hills outside of Los Angeles. It had a ballroom and a tavern in one end or side of it. He had a little band, and on weekends they'd play there at the ballroom. He was a great guy to record with. He had the first million selling #1 record on Capitol; it was "Smoke, Smoke, Smoke That Cigarette" in 1946. He worked a lot of miles off of that one song. I did an early recording with him in '62, we went up to Las Vegas and did a live album at the Mint Club with him singing with Biff Collie who at that time was on KFOX. I thought it would be nice to have a disc jockey on it and make it kinda like a radio show, pitter patter talking like a radio show. We called it "Tex Williams at the Mint Club". It wasn't a big seller, but the disc jockeys liked it. They would put it on and treat it like a fifteen minute radio show. We had a lot of people call and say how much they enjoyed it. Tex Williams was the gentleman of country-western music – he was a genuine gentleman. Everybody felt the same way about him as I did.

I think I told about meeting Bob Wills in Claremore in 1949 on Will Rogers Day. It was a big step in my career to work with Johnnie Lee; actually I was playing that summer up in Wichita, Kansas in 1952 with Jimmy Hall who had been with Leon McAullife. Jimmy had a band at the Cowboy Inn. We had been in a club down in Lawton all of '50 and '51. We worked for a year and a half without a day off – seven days a week, so some of the boys in the band said, "Let's go some where, where we can get a day off". So some of us went to Wichita because Jimmy was starting his band. We worked for him, and it was a lot of fun.

Then Johnnie Lee needed a guitar player. He had called Bill Wimberly; Gene Crownover was playing with Bill Wimberly on a radio show in Wichita, so Gene came out to see me and said, "Do you want to work for Johnnie Lee"? I said, "Yes, I'd love to". They had had some kind of liquor violation at the Club and were to be closed for thirty days, but it could have been six months. The owner said, "If you guys have some place where you can work, you'd better take it". Bill Wimberly called Johnnie Lee and said, "We've got you a guitar player up here", and told him who I was. Johnnie Lee said, "Well, tell him to come on down and be ready to go to work". I came down to Cain's on a Saturday night and played my first job with Johnnie Lee. It was in the fall of '52, and Don Tole had just left. I played that Saturday night dance, and Johnnie Lee said, "I guess you want to go to work with us". I said, "Yeh, I'd love to work with you". He said, "We've got Leon McAullife down the street at the Cimarron Ballroom, and we're here at Cain's. Those guys jump

130

around a lot; Bobby Bruce jumps up in the air, so I guess you could say we've got a more solemn type band". I hung on to that for years; it was a lot of fun.

Back then Bob's and Johnnie Lee's parents, Uncle John and Aunt Emmy Wills, had moved back to Tulsa; Uncle John, who was an old time fiddler, had been down at the Trianon in Oklahoma City with Bob and always had his fiddle plugged into amps. Johnnie Lee didn't amplify his fiddles, and they didn't have pickups on them – they played right into the mike. I was sitting on the left, and Uncle John would come up on my side, hand me the pickup chord and say, "Plug me in there, Slim, and turn that son-of-a-gun up a little so I can hear". He'd get up there and Johnnie Lee would say, "Poppa, got your fiddle"? He'd say, "Yeh"; then he'd hit the strings a couple of times, and Johnnie Lee would look at me with his hand at his side telling me to turn him down a little.

That was in 1952, of course Bob had been out in California a few years, but I was with Johnnie Lee with Henry Boatman, Curly and Cotton Thompson. Curly and Henry would stand with Johnnie Lee in the middle; they'd stand on each side of him and play right into the mike right there at Cain's. The only time Cotton played fiddle was when he would sing, or Johnnie Lee might call him up there to play a solo. He never would play with the fiddlers; they'd play "Liberty" and breakdowns, and I don't remember Cotton ever joining in with them. I think it was on up in the '50s when Johnnie Lee amplified the fiddles; until then they just crowded up to the mike and played. Uncle John was the first amplified fiddler Johnnie Lee let play. That was on the Saturday radio show – every Saturday night.

After I left Johnnie Lee's band, I went back to Lawton to work there at the Southern Club. We hired this kid that just came up to sing; it was

Joe Carson. He was sixteen years old, and we called him Little Joe Carson – he was Little Joe. He was great, and he started to write some songs. Hank Thompson produced the first session with him; it was when Hank was with Capitol. He went to Nashville to do a session; Billy Grey and Wanda Jackson had recorded some duets. He took Little Joe up there and made a deal with Mercury Records for Little

Tommy at his first Austin City Limits Show in 1976, appearing with the Original Texas Playboys; Leon McAuliffe at the microphone and steel guitar.

Joe Carson. Joe stayed with me for several years working around Lawton, Wichita Falls and in Texas. In '58 when I went on the road with Buddy Holly, he was on the band. The last time we played Lawton was after Buddy was killed.

We moved out to Odessa. We worked there awhile, Joe worked with me and then I went on to California. When I took the Country-Western Department, I signed Joe with Liberty and took him up to Nashville and recorded him. We had a pretty good record called "Shoot the Buffalo"; it sold pretty good. Then I brought him out to California and used sort of a California country band and cut a song; actually we cut a whole album while he was out there. We had a couple of hits off of that album. As I said earlier he was killed in a car wreck in Wichita Falls; he had a great career ahead of him – a great country singer. I go back now and listen

132

JULIE ANDREWS SESSION. *To Tom -*
NASHVILLE, TENN. *With my love & thanks*
JUNE 5 1978 *Julie Andrews.*

Tommy played bass guitar on the June 5, 1978, Julie Andrews session in Nashville;
Tommy has the cowboy hat and Julie Andrews is the third person to his left.

to some of that old stuff we cut with him. I had Glenn Campbell singing
harmony with him. Glenn said, "He's one of the purest country singers
I've ever heard in my life".

The Statler Brothers and the Oak Ridge Boys, I did sessions with both
of those groups. The Statler Brothers were from that old school; they just
walked in and sang it live. The Oak Ridge Boys were the same way; they
just came in and nailed it. I can see how the new singers can envy people
like that. Now they have to tune them up; you go back and listen to these
old records and there was no tuning up in those days.

I did a lot of sessions with Johnny Cash in the '70s. He was always
really nice; he had some of his guys, a drummer, piano player and a guitar

player, would be there. He would off set his band with studio musicians. He was always really nice to everybody and the same with his wife. I enjoyed recording with them.

I did a couple of Gene Watson sessions, and I was leader and arranger. "Love on a Hot Afternoon" was the first session, and it was a hit. Then we did "Paper Roses", and it was a #1 hit. Then he came in with a song "An Old Man with a Horn" about an old man in New Orleans with a horn. I said, "If you do a song like this, you have to have a trumpet on it". So we bring in a trumpet; we still had all the same guys who had been playing on all his hits. So we cut the song, and it was pretty aggressive up to #1. Then someone at Capitol said, "You need a producer on this; you've got Tommy Allsup doing all of the arranging. He's produced Asleep at the Wheel for Capitol and the Texas Playboys; your records sound like theirs". The only reason it had a western sound on it was because it had a horn. So the next time he came in, he didn't call me. He had two #1 records and one that almost was #1, but someone had put a bug in his ear that I was going to make a western swing star out of him, which wouldn't have hurt. He sang on the last Texas Playboy album; he sang "Lilly Dale" and did a great job on it.

Eldon told me that a song would be written and usually copyrighted in Bob's name, so Tommy Duncan volunteered to take the package or envelope to the post office for Bob. On the way he would open it and add his name; that was part of the trouble between Bob and Tommy. Eldon said that he knew that Bob wrote "Eight Weeks Ago Tonight We Parted", because one night he held the flashlight while Bob wrote it on the hood of his car. They were coming back from a job up north – maybe Hominy, and Bob stopped the car. He asked him if he had paper and a pencil; he had a tablet. Eldon kept a record of what the band played, so Bob put it on the hood and wrote the words to "Eight Weeks Ago Tonight We Parted" (*the first line in "I Wonder If You Feel the Way I Do"*). He said, "Tommy didn't write that" and "Bob wrote those songs". Bob told me that; when I cut the first album I produced with him, Bob would get behind the steering wheel and run off the road. He would get so mad thinking about Tommy; I think they were both responsible for that sound. Tommy is as responsible as Bob, but they just ended up hating each other.

I was getting a lot of rock and roll sessions back in the early '60s. I would call Glenn Campbell; we became good friends and would go camping together down on Lake Havasu. We had a lot of fun back in those days. I recorded the Everly Brothers in California after they got out of the Marines in the early '60s. They already had their big hits and moved to California and signed with Warner Brothers Records. I had a good friend with Warner Records, and he called me and said, "Do you want to be a leader on the session"? I said, "Yeh, I'd love to". He put together a band to record with them. I think Leon Russell was on piano. Jerry Allison played the drums – he had been Buddy Holly's drummer. James Burton, Glenn Campbell – we had a really good band. Everybody was good there at the studio. They had a producer from Warner Brothers; they had Lou Addler who had produced the "Mamas and the Papas" and all that good stuff, and then we had Don and Phil calling the shots. The first day we had two sessions; the time was spent arguing over who was going to do what. I have never been in such a battle in my life with so many people trying to run a session. The second day after everyone got over being mad it was great to cut with them. They were amazing talent, and once they decided to record it, it was done.

Merle Haggard – I met Merle when I had Little Joe Carson on Liberty Records. Merle was up in Las Vegas playing bass in Wynn Stewart's band

Tommy Allsup and Clint Eastwood in 1982; Tommy played the guitar in Eastwood's movie, HONKYTONK MAN.

in a club called Nashville West. His manager had gone in with him and recorded "Sing Me a Sad Song". Wynn Stewart had written the song, and Merle recorded. They were pitching it around to different labels trying to get a label interested in it. I had just recorded Joe Carson, and I was kind of in the same style. I got to hear that song before he signed with Capitol. Capitol put it out, and he started his string of hits. He has written so many great songs. When I did *For the Last Time* album, Merle was there when I put it together. He came into the room and Cindy Walker and I had gone over to see Bob. Cindy told Bob, "You've got some songs you've been holding of mine". Bob said, "I know that". One was "What Makes Bob Holler"?; he had "Goin' Away Party", "When You Leave Amarillo (Turn Out the Lights)", "Baby, That Sure Would Be Good" – Leon McAuliffe sang it. Cindy had given them to him somewhere down the line; she had written so many of his songs. He had just been packing them around with him. Merle said that he sure would like to be a part of it. Bob said, "You

136

sure can; can't he, Tommy"? I said, "If he works for scale he can". Merle said, "I'll be a Texas Playboy for a day playing for union scale". So he came in, and that's what happened. When we were recording "Bob Wills 100th Birthday" I called Merle and said, "Would you do "Misery" on this album"? He said, "Have you cut the tracks on it yet"? I said, "No, but we can do it and send them to you; you can come back here and put the vocals on". He said, "If you'll do the tracks just like the original record and let me play Bob's fiddle part". On the original they play in D and then go up to E, just like they did on "Faded Love". Then Bob plucks the A sting, and they play it in A; then Tommy Duncan came in to sing and put a little tag on it. It starts off with twin guitars. I left the fiddle part open, sent it out to California, and he sang it and put the fiddle in. He was playing the same fiddle that Bob played. He has that fiddle. I told a disc jockey or two that he said that he would play the fiddle part on Bob's own fiddle. I played with Carl Perkins; he was always on Johnny Cash's sessions. He was a fine guy; I had met him before. I was playing the Silver Saddle Club down in Odessa in the winter of '58. We had come off that fall tour with Buddy; Buddy came in there to plan the January session we did in February. Carl had played at the Silver Saddle, and I told him we had come off of a tour with Buddy; we had just done the biggest rock and roll show of the year. Carl was a nice guy; he was genuine, simple as milk, and another original.

Marty Robbins was another nice man; I always enjoyed him. I met him when I first moved to Nashville. I had met him in the early '50s when his first record came out; we were playing the Southern Club in Lawton in about '53. He came in there and played; Tommy Hill played guitar with him, and Goldy Hill was the star of the show. Marty was sort of a backup on the Goldy Hill Show. He would get up there and sing his heart out, but

Tommy with Hank Thompson in 1976 while he played rhythm guitar and produced Hank's album for Dot Records, Back in the Swing of Things.

he couldn't say a word. He couldn't even say, "Hello, Friends". He couldn't introduce his next song he was so shy. We talked about this in the '70s when I was in Nashville; he said, "I was shy. One night at the Grand Ole Opry they asked if I could play the piano, and I just sat down and started talking. I got away from that shyness if I was playing the piano; I had to learn to talk when I had a guitar". He used to close the Opry; he had the 11:00 to 12:00 spot, and WSM just let him go as long as he wanted to go. It would spill over into the Ernest Tubb Record Shop; sometimes he would go thirty minutes over. He turned into one heck of an entertainer. We made the sound track for the movie *HONKYTONK MAN*, starring Clint Eastwood, and they gave him a prop-guitar to play while he was singing. Back at the hotel he said, "We're gonna shoot my scene tomorrow; what kind of guitar you got with you"? I said, "I've got a Martin". He said, "Can I borrow it"? I said, "You sure can", and he takes my guitar and plays it when he takes over in the studio scene. The next day we recorded

138

the radio scene where Clint comes to see Bob Wills; I'm playing that same guitar that Marty had used. They gave him a prop-guitar the kind that we called little Gene Autry guitars; it had a little picture of Gene on it. The strings were about three quarters of an inch high. He said, "I can't even make an open chord on that thing". Marty was a good guy and a great talent.

Hank Thompson – I met Hank in 1950, and I started producing his albums for ABC Records in the mid-1970s. They hired me to do a bunch of albums with him. Hank was good. We all played at the party when Hank passed away; he didn't want a funeral, just a big party and get all his friends there singing. They had it at Billy Bob's in Fort Worth. Mel Tillis came out from Nashville to sing and brought part of his band with him. It was a great afternoon of entertaining, and his wife, Ann, said, "That's what he wanted – 'just invite all my friends and drink a little wine for me'". That was his send off – a whole afternoon of entertainment.

Slim Whitman – Liberty bought out the label Imperial – Slim Whitman had been there his whole career. Just before I left Liberty they asked if I would produce an album on Slim Whitman. We called the album *Country Songs City Hits*; they were country songs that had gone over into the pop field like "A Little Bitty Tear Let Me Down" and songs in that gender. I asked him if he wanted to cut it in Nashville; he said, "No, the musicians in Nashville make fun of me". I thought that was kind of odd, for here's a man who has had million sellers. He said, "I like to record in Dallas, and I like Marvin Montgomery there at the Burnett Studio". I met him in Dallas up the road from the studio. Usually 10:00 is a good time to start; I said, "Slim, what time do you want to start tomorrow"? He said, "Well I like to sing about six o'clock". I said, "You start singing about 6:00, and I'll meet you about 10:00; the bands coming in about 10:00". He said, "I like to walk about three or four miles before I sing". I said, "Good, go at it". He was a health guy; he didn't smoke and didn't drink. That's the only album I did with him.

I worked with Vince Gill on the "Asleep at the Wheel" project; we did "Bob's Break Down". Vince Gill, Steve Wariner and I won a Grammy for that instrumental in the year 2000. Vince is really a good old Oklahoma boy; he plays the heck out of the guitar and sings great.

I met Ray Price when I was working the Southern Club in the early '50s. We stayed friends through the years. When I moved up to Nashville in '68, it was in early '69 I had a guy named Clay Hart, we had a hit called "Spring". I was looking for a follow up, and Kris Kristofferson gave me a demo with some of his songs on it. It was a disc; they cut them on a disc. We went through it, and there was one song there – "For the Good Times". Clay didn't like it. I said, "Clay, I think that's a hit song". Clay said, "He's got an up tempo song, and I sure want to do one of Kris's songs". I said, "Okay". So Mary Jon Wilkens, the publisher, said, "Tommy, Ray Price is in town recording; would you take it to Ray"? I said, "Sure". I had an office right behind Columbia Studios. I go over there, and Curley Chalker was playing steel. Cam Mullins writing all the string parts on it. I took Ray that song, "For the Good Times". They took a break; I handed him that demo and a set of lyrics, and said, "I think that's a hit song for you". He said, "Well, let's go up to Frank Jones' office and listen to it". Frank was Ray's producer. Frank said, "I really like that song". I said, "I do too". He said, "Cam, write the charts for it, and we'll do it tomorrow". Clay Hart later became a great singing star for the Lawrence Welk Show, and every time I would see him I'd say, "Clay, I sure am glad you didn't cut that song, because Ray Price needed a hit at that time".

I had Vikki Carr as a country-western artist in my roster. Snuffy

Garrett had a country singer in his roster. So he said that we need to switch. I had used her sometimes as a backup singer with Bob Wills. On Bob Wills Sings and Plays (Liberty LST-7303), he said, "Tommy, get me a vocal backup group; I want some pretty singing behind me". He was going to do a lot of the singing. We did "Rosetta", "Yearning", "Will You Miss Me When I'm Gone"; he said, "I want you to get a girl singer who can hit them high notes – way up there – sound like an angel". I told Vikki about that; I had her and Billy Mize and Cliff Crawford – I was producing them at that time. We went in to do background with Bob, and it was the first time he had had background singers. We are doing a song, and Vikki goes in and hits a high note. Back in those days we were cutting on three tracks – Bob's fiddle and the vocal in the middle with two outside tracks. He hollered, "Yaaaaahhhhhh". The engineer said, "Look here, all three needles just flopped over there in red; Tommy, I don't know how I'm going to get that holler out". You couldn't edit back then like you can now; "Snap Your Fingers" was the name of the song. Bob was a one take only; he would say, "Boys, we've been playing this song for twenty years; Luke, you been singin' it for twenty-five years. We don't need to sit up here and play it a half dozen times; we're going to play it one time, and you better get it". We did it one time, and that was it.

Luke sings "Will You Miss Me When I'm Gone"?; we play it back and listen to it. I'm playing guitar on the session, and I'm listening on headphones. You miss a few little things like that. Sam Gibbs, his manager sitting in the Control Room, said, "That's a good take". Bob said, "That's a good take, Luke; you sing it really good". I said, "Sam, we really need to make one more take on that; Bob's fiddle is a little flat. Will you tell him"? Sam said, "No, Tommy, I'm not going to tell him; you're the producer – you go out there and tell him". I said, "No, let's just leave it

Tommy's Heads Up Saloon, Dallas.

alone". It's not that bad, and Bob liked it.

Tanya Tucker was thirteen years old when she came to Nashville; her momma brought her. She had been up to Las Vegas, and she had picked up this manager who knew somebody that knew somebody – it was one of those kind of deals. I talked to Billy Sherrill who was a producer there at Columbia; he said, "Watch this little girl coming in; she's a friend of this publisher in New York . He's telling us she can do this and that, and I'm going to try her. I don't know; the only song I've got for her is about a hooker in New Orleans, and she's only thirteen years old. I don't know what I'm going to do". I said, "Just go tell her". So Tanya's first record was "Delta Dawn"; she's thirteen years old and got a hit. I worked with her all through her Columbia years; she was good, and we stayed friends. She sang on our last Playboy album. She would drop by when she came through town; we've been good buddies all these years. She still sings as good or better than she ever did. I saw her at Billy Bob's, and she had it packed – 5,000 people or more. She has a list of songs, probably twenty-five hit songs; she can go out and do a show with just her hits. People don't realize that she had that many hits. Barbara Mandrell was another I recorded with when I was out in California; she was on the *Town Hall Party* in the late '50s.

Johnny Burnette had some hits back in the '60s – "Sweet Sixteen". Back in the '50s Johnny was about the first rock and roll before Elvis. Elvis used to watch Johnny Burnette and his brother Dorsey and the guitar player, Paul Burleson. Johnny had a son, Rocky; Dorsey had a son named Billy. Even Carl Perkins said that he believed that's where the term rockabilly came from – the Johnny Burnette Trio. They were before Bill Haley, before Elvis – they were doing the same things Elvis was doing. He was a big buddy of Elvis's. He's the one who took me up to that big party at Elvis's in Beverly Hills. Johnny Burnette was great. Even on his Liberty records you can hear a little of that rockabilly influence; he went back to the very beginning of it.

I worked with Snuffy Garrett who produced Gene McDaniels' "A Hundred Pounds of Clay" which became a hit. One day we were sitting there in Liberty and Gene came in and told Snuff he wanted to do a jazz album with a jazz trio. Snuffy said that he didn't know anything about jazz. Gene had three number #1 records, but he wanted his contract back. He just wanted to sing jazz.

There were a couple of young kids out in California, Jan and Dean, during the surf music days. One was studying to be a doctor at UCLA; the other was studying at Southern Cal. They decided one day that they wanted to sing some rock and roll, so they got hold of Lou Adler, a friend of theirs, and started making records. Later one of them, I think Jan, had a car wreck. We did a little surfing music with them like "Dead Man's Curve" and "The Little Old Lady from Pasadena"; they were a big influence on what I call surf music or whatever the Beach Boys were doing.

The Ventures were on a label that Liberty owned, Dalton Records. They had a string of hits, but when the twist came out the band had kind of broken up. The guitarist Nokie Edwards, the lead guitar player and from Oklahoma, had left them. They wanted to finish a twist album; they got me and Jerry Allison, the Crickets drummer who was out there at that time, so we finished that twist album. I wrote a song called "Bluer Than Blue" (on *The Colourful Ventures* Dalton BST-8008, 1961) and when we recorded it, we used some strings on it; it became a big record. They got back together when Nokie returned.

Del Shannon already had a big hit on "Run Away" and had moved to California. We did a lot of studio work with him. He was a nice guy who knew exactly what he wanted, and the album that had an organ on it became a popular hit. There's much written about Leon Russell; I met him when he first came to California with David Gates. I got him his first job; it was a Sunday night at the Palomino Club. I had used him on some demo sessions and record sessions, and about the time I left there was about the time he started producing things on his own.

Jerry Lee Lewis was always fun to record with; he'd come into Nashville doing a lot of country music. The songwriter Glenn Sutton had been married to Lynn Anderson. I played on a lot of Jerry Lee's country songs, and when he cut "What Made Milwaukee Famous", Glenn was supposed to have a song ready for him that night. The night before the session, his producer, Jerry Kennedy, called and said, "Do you have that song ready for Jerry Lee; he's coming in tomorrow to cut it". Glenn had just brought in a six pack of Milwaukee Beer, and he was sitting at the table and said, "Yes, I've got one started, and I'll finish it tonight". Jerry

Lee's producer said, "What's the name of it"? He looked at the label and said, "'What Made Milwaukee Famous (Made a Loser Out of Me)'". The producer said, "That sounds good to me; can Jerry Lee come down and look at it"? He said, "No, wait 'til I get it finished; I'll bring it down tomorrow". He worked it into the session the next day, and Jerry Lee learned it – a number #1 hit. Jerry Lee was always a lot of fun. It was like watching one of his shows; you never knew what was going to happen in the studio. They had two pianos, and he always had Pig Robbins playing one.

Back in the late '50s they'd bring Screaming Jay Hawkins out on the stage in a coffin; he'd raise up out of the coffin. That was his gimmick, and he came to Nashville to record in the '70s. The producer thought it would be funny if the studio had him in a coffin. So we all go out to Woodland Sound Studio, a big studio, and there was a coffin in the studio. It was open about an inch or two. I knew what his rock and roll days were, but I didn't say anything. The musicians were all in their places, and he kicked that casket open, jumped up and screamed "Screaming Jay Hawkins". It was funny, but the worst thing to do in a session.

Buddy Knox started out the same place Buddy Holly did – at Norman Petty's Studio in Clovis, New Mexico; I later hooked up with him out in California, and we did a lot of sessions. The Fleetwoods were two girls and a guy out of the state of Washington. I did a country album with Andy Williams in Nashville; Andy Williams is a super nice man. I did a bunch of projects with Julie London in the early Liberty days; she was a Liberty Artist, and in the mid-'50s had one of the first hits with "Cry Me a River" with just Barney Kessel and a bass player. She was good to work with. I did several sessions with Bobby Vinton in Nashville. Eydie Gorme and Steve Lawrence were fun, and Julie Andrews was a big hit because she came down to Nashville to cut an album in the '70s when her husband was doing those Pink Panther movies. She said that he was going to fly in to watch a session, and he did fly in on the second night just to come to a session. She was really good and fun.

Another kind of odd ball session was Mae West. She had a big session; her agent called me and said that we would be recording Mae West. We get to the studio and there are about twenty violin string players, horns and a rhythm section all in the same room. In the studio there was a big punch bowl, real crystal for the champagne or wine; it was her thing. Just before she came in they would pour the champagne. She came in with these big old guys, big muscled guys, that were her stick back then. She came walking in; she said "Hello" to everybody, and everybody had to get a cup and toast her – a toast to start her album. It almost looked like a Broadway Play instead of an album. We had everything all set and everybody set a certain way and "You all be kinda dressed". It was a fun session; the album came out, but I've never heard that album. I've tried to find a copy, but haven't. It wasn't a big hit, but for me it was just fun to be on it. I was a big fan.

I played on Jack Jones first session. We cut a song, "Lollipops and Roses", and he just hated it. He said, "I'm just not into this kid stuff; I want to sing pop music". His Dad had been an opera singer, Alan Jones. They tried to get him into the rock field, but he wanted to sing pop. From that time on he just cut with the big bands.

Chapter 9
LOOKING BACK

Larry Scott, Tommy's close friend and member of the Disc Jockey Hall of Fame, recalled, *"There has never been a producer like Tommy. You take all these old guys on the For the Last Time album – Hoyle Nix and all the old timers – the companionship was great, but also a distraction because they wanted to visit so much. It was an inspiration that came out on the record, too. But it was the producer who had to put it all together. We were standing there listening to the play back of "Big Balls in Cow Town" and bragging to Hoyle Nix, who is credited with that version. He said, 'I don't know if it will ever make it or not; I wore out four fiddles, four busses, and four wives.' On that Monday, the third of December (1973), it was about 12:00 or 12:30 when Betty rolled Bob through those double doors at Sumet-Bernet Studios. Those old cats were having a great time cuttin' up, and when Betty rolled The Old Man in, they snapped to attention. It was just like it was when he stepped on the band stand. It was like a general walking in and saying, 'Attention.' And it took Tommy to put it together and to make it jell.*

"I always thank Tommy for making it possible for me to meet some of these old musicians. It's what we always dream of and hope for, and he made it possible for me. I grew up in the western part of Missouri, and I grew up listening to Johnnie Lee – Bob had already gone. Then Leon came out after World War II on KRMG. It was a ritual to come in out of the field and hear Glen Condon do the news, then the Trumpeteers Quartette; Leon, and Johnnie Lee".

"On October 24, 1976, in San Antonio, Bobbie Barker, the Farmer's Daughter, was having her anniversary show and wanted the Playboys. It was being broadcast over a small station, and Leon McAuliffe would get nervous and lose his voice – he needed help. We would play the theme song and he would lose his voice. I was down there with them and introduced them. It may have been the first night that Bob Boatright worked with the Playboys. Jack Stidham came down with Keith Coleman. The next day was when Tommy produced their first Capitol album – Leon had already fired Gimble and was using Jack Stidham. After that was over, Capitol wanted to do a radio program, a public relations show. Tommy put it together; they recorded twelve hours that day, on Tuesday. We got them to tell some stories. Recorded it on two tracks, and it turned out great.

One significant thing about that album is that it was the last time Keith Coleman played with the Playboys before he died. And Leon Rausch yodeled on it singing 'Gambling Polka Dot Blues.' Tommy took Asleep At the Wheel into the KRLD Studio and recorded 'Fat Boy Rag.' Capitol released it, and it was great".

Maria Elena, Buddy's wife was a secretary at Southern Music, the publisher that was handling all of Norman Petty's catalog which was basically Buddy Holly songs. The first time Buddy saw her, he said he was going to marry her.

After Buddy was killed, she dropped out of the picture and married a guy who was ambassador from Puerto Rico or something. They raised a family. She was out of the picture for years, and then the Buddy Holly movie appears and she's the technical advisor. They didn't talk to the Holly family, to any of The Crickets – she took over. That's why no one really liked the movie – they didn't even mention the Norman Petty

Part of Tommy's band, 1987; Tommy Morrell, steel guitar; Tommy Allsup, guitar;
Lanny Long, bass; Bob Boatright, fiddle.

Studio in Clovis where all of his early hits were cut. There were a lot of things they left out of the movie – it was not correct!! She came back into the picture after raising a family with another man, and they split up – she's living in Irving, Texas. I didn't see her again until 1987.

I had a club in Fort Worth, Texas from 1980 until 1987, when we shut it down. I was opening a club in Dallas called "Tommy's Heads Up Saloon" – I knew the movie was coming out and that it was kinda tied in with the movie La Bamba.

We were playing at a little supper club on the north side of Dallas. This guy who owned it, Dick Chase, was sorta off the wall. He had had a successful club on the west side of Dallas called "Dick's Last Resort". Well, he built this place called the "Chase Lounge" and Tex Whitson (Merle Haggard's ex-manager) set up a meeting, and Chase said, "Yeh, Let's put some western swing in on Thursday's".

Tommy Allsup, Jr., with Paul McCartney and Jerry Allison at the opening of the Buddy Holly stage show, New York City, 1991.

The "Let's Ride with Bob" session, Garland, Texas, 1992, WR Records; l to r: Rich O'Brien, Bill Carson, Tommy Allsup, Craig Chambers, Bobby Koefer, and Tommy Morrell, seated.

The Bob Wills' Texas Playboys, Labor Day, 1995, Jefferson, Texas, Fair.

Performing at the Lincoln County Cowboy Symposium, Glencoe, New Mexico;
l to r: Curly Lewis, fiddle; Snuffy Elmore, fiddle; Frankie Mc Whorter, fiddle; Craig
Chambers, bass; Tommy Allsup, guitar.

The Texas Playboys performing at the Nevada Palace, Las Vegas, Nevada, for the National Finals Rodeo, 1992; l to r: Curly Lewis, fiddle; Luke Wills, vocalist; Leon Rausch, bass; Tommy Allsup, guitar.

Two Guitar Legends: Tommy Allsup and Eldon Shamblin performing at the Lincoln County Cowboy Symposium, Glencoe, New Mexico.

152

Tom Morrell, Bob Boatright, and I had put a little group together; we had a good band. People who usually wouldn't go to the clubs came when they would hear that we were playing there on Thursday nights. So we got the wild idea of going down to "Deep Elum" and building "Tommy's Heads Up Saloon" and having western swing three or four nights a week and bringing in stars the other nights.

Maria Elena shows up one night at the "Chase Lounge" like a long lost sister – hugs my neck and was so glad to see me. I stayed with Buddy and Maria Elena at their apartment in New York. There never was any mention of her being pregnant. On the Winter Dance Party Tour, Buddy didn't say a word to me about it, and everyday the Big Bopper talked about his wife being pregnant. Not one word from Buddy was mentioned to me or Waylon about his wife being pregnant.

Ritchie Valens was only 17. He was a good guitar player, a good singer who had a big career ahead of him. After the tour, I moved to California in the early part of '60. I tried to find his mother, but they had moved on up the coast. His sister Connie, later in 1994, told me that I was the last link to her brother, and I wanted to talk with his mother. His sister was only six when he was killed, and she said she remembered that he used to do the dishes for their mother. "He would put us up on a chair and we would dry them". She said that they heard I had quit music because I had flipped that coin and went on the bus and he got killed, that it had torn me up so much that I went off in the hills and wouldn't talk to people. I told her that I had tried to find them. She said that they had tried to find me to let me know that there were no hard feelings, it was just something that happened. I was leery about what I was going to say because it had been thirty-five years. It was the thirty-fifth anniversary when I saw her. She said, "I want you to know that no one in the family

153

feels bad about you for flipping that coin". We became friends, but it had always been in the back of my mind that they would resent me – what would they say? What could I have said to his mother, "I flipped the coin, and he's dead and I'm alive"? I was twenty-eight when it happened. Buddy was twenty-two. The Bopper was probably in his late twenties; he would get phone calls at night and say, "Hellooo, Baby, this is the Big Bopper". That was his way of talking to people – just like the record. He wrote "White Lightening" for George Jones, and I believe George gave him a ballad he had written. He was a good song writer.

I've made a good living in music; I recorded with all the good people. The rock song, "In the Year 2525", sold nine million copies; the album sold two million. I had already moved to Nashville when it was released and became a hit. It was the biggest record of the year around the world in '69, but I was already in Nashville.

I had moved to Nashville, but we kept the studio open in Odessa. We put the record out on our label. We had an order for 5,000 out of Minneapolis. They called RCA, and the RCA guy came by and called Zager and Evans and asked who had the masters. My ex-brother-in-law and I had a fifty-fifty percent contract with Zager and Evans. We furnished the studio and musicians, and they furnished the talent. We published the songs, and split every thing down the middle. Me being in Nashville and they being in Minneapolis with the RCA guy – my brother-in-law came to Nashville and said, "We should have published that song". Well, I remember the day we had the lead sheet made and sent in the copyright papers. It was one of those brother-in-law deals where they laid some bread on him. I could have called the copyright office, and should have, but I was going through a divorce with his wife's sister. I was so pissed off about the divorce. He said that I would either buy him out or he would buy me out for my half of the studio. I was so mad that I said, "Give me a dollar". He went across the street and had a lawyer draw up the papers. We owned the land and the studio, but I just wanted to get rid of it because he had screwed me once. It wasn't that important to me.

Zager and Evans weren't men enough to come to Nashville and look me in the eye and say, "We want you to help us on the album". I put the damn song together for them; I played guitar and bass on it and over dubbed the strings and horns on it. I made the song what it was, and we put it out. I just didn't care to work with them, because they weren't willing to come by and say "This song is a hit, and you're in for some money". Instead, they got greedy. But that was the only hit they ever had. I could have called them and said, "If you had come back to me, we might have put together another hit". But with RCA Victor, they couldn't buy a hit. They got the money, but I got the laugh.

I met Janis Joplin in Nashville in 1969. She was a good friend of one of my Metromedia Records' Artists – Alex Harvey. He brought her by my office when she was in Nashville doing a show. I really became a bigger fan of hers after meeting her and talking with her – a phenomenal talent. I've been blessed to have met and talked with a lot of big stars, including Frank Sinatra, Dean Martin, Steve Allen, Ella Fitzgerald and many others.

In the mid '60's, after I opened my recording studio in Odessa, I met Herbert Graham. Herb wanted me to help him produce a young singer from Eastland, Texas. We cut some songs for him and took them out to Hollywood to play for Jimmy Bowen, who was running Reprise Records. He loved the singer and gave us a budget to record six songs. He was looking for a hit single, so we got busy cutting the songs. After we delivered the songs, Bowen wanted the singer and his band to come to his home in Brentwood and perform there for him. Well, he loved the singer and loved the band! So that evening, to celebrate, we went to hear a young black blues singer and rip-it-up guitar player at The Cave in Hollywood, a trendy club at that time. We listened in amazement to JIMI HENDRIX. I met and talked with him between sets, and he was a great guy! Oh, by the way, our singer was Teddy Neeley, who later played the lead in *Jesus Christ Superstar.*

Monument to Buddy Holly, Ritchie Valens, J. P. "The Big Bopper" Richardson, and Roger Peterson (the pilot), Surf Ballroom, Clear Lake, Iowa.

Around 1971 Columbia Records was having a worldwide convention in London. They took some studio musicians along to play behind one of their C&W musicians, Johnny Paycheck. The band was made up of me, Pete Drake, Henry Strzlechi, Jerry Carrigan and George Ritchey.

Pete and I were sitting in the lobby of the famous Grosvenor House Hotel and in walked three of the Beatles – John, George and Ringo. Ringo, with whom Pete had cut the song "Act Naturally" in his studio in Nashville, had come by to see Pete. It was cool talking with those three guys.

I met Sir Paul McCartney in the early 1990's. He had me and The Texas Playboys play for his End of The World Tour in Chicago. When Leon Rausch told Paul, "This is Tommy Allsup", Paul said, "I know who he is; he's one of my heros". It was not too long after that that I worked

Statue of Buddy Holly at the Civic Center, Lubbock, Texas.

with Paul in New York – he is truly a gentleman.

I have had big cars, nice homes and gone where I wanted to go. So my life in music has been good. I did more than just play the guitar to make a living in music; I know great musicians who are starving to death. I had talent in the studio, and that's what I really like to do – to get in the studio and put things together, record songs. I've been a producer, an arranger, an A & R man; I've found the songs and have found the artists. I've done every thing from A to Z in the music business. Playing the

Tommy with Lorrie Morgan and Ron Gaddis following a recording session in Nashville, 1999.

guitar helped, and I've recorded with Willie Nelson, Charlie Rich, George Jones, Tammy Wynette and other greats such as Mae West and Julie Andrews.

It seems that the really big stars are the easiest to record; Julie Andrews just walked in and sang. No problems at all. The "want to be" and "like to be stars" can give you hell, and the ones who didn't quite make it are resentful. They believe that the studio musicians didn't or don't play as well as they do with a big star. Well, "Hell, No", with attitudes like that you don't play as well. I have always believed that you have to have the right attitude to work with people.

They didn't give musicians credit until the '70s, so I'm not mentioned on many albums. When I started recording, the union scale was $41.25 per session; in fact, Joe Carson's Capitol sessions in 1956 paid the $41.25 union scale. It's over $300 now, and the leader gets double. The union has a scale for everything now days.

Tommy in October, 1998 holding a fifty cent piece at the door in Clear Lake, Iowa where he flipped the coin on February 2, 1959.

I'm kind of like an outlaw in Nashville, because I like swing. They see me coming and say, "Aw, Oh, here comes old western swing". When I was running record labels they called me Mr. Allsup, now they say, "Here comes Mr. Western Swing". Johnny Gimble said that he thought WSM meant "Wrong Side of the Mississippi"; to me it means "Western Swing Music".

Today if I were doing western swing music, I would try to find a good comfortable studio, for western has to be live. You have to set everyone up in a circle where they can hear one another play. You can set up each musician in a separate room and record that way, but you lose the feel. I remember Dallas; that's where we recorded *For the Last Time*, and Leon Rausch and I did our tribute to Bob Wills there. I did two Asleep at the Wheel albums there, but that studio is closed so I don't know where I would go. If I were going to do a country recording, I'd go to Nashville

– that's where the great country sounds are recorded.

I mentioned that I learned to play the fiddle when I was a kid. Well, when I had my own bands, if we didn't have a fiddler in the band sometimes I would play some breakdowns or round dances – "Faded Love", "Maiden's Prayer". Then Louie Tierney started teaching me in 1957; I traded him an old car for a fiddle. I gave that fiddle to the museum out in Canyon, Texas. It was a pretty good fiddle; Bob had put it in a shop down in Fort Worth to be worked on, and Louie got it out of the shop. He played it two or three years, and I swapped him an old convertible there in Lawton for it. That's the one he shot the top out of in Hobbs, New Mexico. He and Mancel were going on a rabbit hunt; he borrowed a shotgun, and you know he and his brother drank a lot all the time. Mancel said, "Brouth, that gun's not loaded is it"? They called each other "Brouth". Louie answered back saying, "Brouth, you think I'm stupid enough to be walkin' aroun' with a loaded gun"? Louie was kind'da crippled and stepped in the car with the gun between his legs and "Boom"! He blew a hole big enough to put a wash tub through in the top of that convertible. They put a piece of paper or something over that hole and drove around for a long time – never did get it fixed. That was about the extent of my fiddle playing. Occasionally, Buddy Spicher and I will be sitting around, and I'll pick up one of his and play something. But I'm not that good; I decided that I should be a guitar and bass player, not a fiddler.

In Lubbock, there was the Cotton Club. It's where Bob Wills, Hank Thompson and others played. A big old metal building with a big dance floor with a fairly nice stage – that's where Buddy saw Elvis Presley for the first time. He told me that when he saw Elvis he decided to try a different kind of music. He wrote "That'll Be The Day" after he saw a John Wayne movie "The Searchers". Buddy and Jerry Allison were at the

Tommy leading the Texas Playboys in Cain's Ballroom, Tulsa, 2010.

movie and heard the line "That'll Be The Day"; Buddy said that it would be a good song title. If you go check Buddy's songs, they all have two or three people as writers. After you're dead, there's not much you can do about someone sticking his name on a song as a co-writer.

I was recording with Don McLean in '77 or '78 when I got my wallet back from the sheriff in Clear Lake. We had just recorded "It Doesn't Matter Anymore" (the last song Buddy recorded). We broke for a lunch break; I went to the post office and opened the box and there's a package with my wallet from Clear Lake, Iowa. I went back and showed Don McLean. I said, "Isn't it strange that we're working on a Buddy song, and I receive my wallet". He puts out "American Pie", and I walk back into the session with my wallet that Buddy was carrying in his pocket. They kept all of that stuff locked up, and when John Goldrosen was writing his book and interviewed me in Nashville, he had gone through the stuff and

TA
Tommy Allsup
Signature Series

In 1999 Samick Guitars issued a limited edition Tommy Allsup Signature Guitar similar in design to the Gibson L5 – only 500 were produced. It has a spruce top and birds eye maple back and is very popular.

asked why they still had my wallet. The deputies said that they had lost contact with me after it came time to release it. He told them that he had just been with me in Nashville and showed them my card. That's why it came to the post office box. I talked to Don in 1994 in Clear Lake, and he said that he thought he had dreamed it. That got to me. He said, "Don't tell that anymore; it's too spooky". He had dreamed about me getting my wallet back. It's in the Hard Rock Cafe in Dallas, in a nice little walnut glass case. It has my 1958 fishing license, 1958 driver's license, and my daughter Gayla's picture. Waylon had drawn $20 the night before, and I had his I. O. U. in it. Buddy had started his label Prizm Records, so I had his business card in it. They move the wallet around to different locations.

The Hard Rock people offered me $30,000 for my guitar that I played on the tour, because Buddy had one just like it – a 1958 Fender Stratocaster, the sunburst finish. The Fender Company gave Buddy and me two of them when we started the 1958 Summer Tour. I had a friend in California who, when I told him I was working with Buddy Holly, said that they needed to get some instruments to us. They sent two guitars and two amps. But someone stole Buddy's guitar and my amp out of the trailer in East St. Louis when we started the tour. On the first few days I couldn't back him up in his part of the show because we just had the one guitar until he had one shipped in from New York. It was identical except of course for the serial numbers. Some thief has Buddy Holly's guitar. The amp was a Fender Bassman amp; later we took out the four speakers – put two in a cabinet and two in another cabinet – made a public address system and used the amplifier part for a brain. A man in Odessa may still have them.

When Leon Rausch and I played Las Vegas, we put on our advertising "Former Texas Playboys" not "Former members of Bob Wills' Texas

Playboys"; Luke came out and said, "I'm a Wills, and you put Bob's name up there". We said, "He still has a widow back in Texas, and she tells us what to do". She got mad at Johnny Gimble and Larry Scott once for using Bob's name without her permission.

One night Leon McAuliffe, Al Strickland, and some others were talking about the early days in Tulsa when everyone who came to a dance got drunk, and their crowd wasn't doing anything the others weren't doing. They said that there was a house of ill repute on First Street – the May Rooms – and there was a grocery store across the street. You would go buy groceries, and those gals would be sitting in the windows with their bras showing. It apparently had been a little hotel, and the woman who owned it, her name was May, was really a big fan of Bob's. She liked him, and he would go there to sober up when he pulled a big drunk. Herman Arnspiger, Bob's first partner, would take him and pick him up. Herman's new wife didn't like for him to do this, so Herman quit the Playboys.

Bob told me once when we were driving across country that when he was sick in Tulsa and the band was at the Golden Nugget, the Nugget had paid them and Tommy had taken the money home with him. The normal procedure was that they wired the money to Betty and she wrote the checks to pay the band. She hadn't received the money, and Bob was mad. He said that he called Tommy at home and told him that "I'm deathly scared of flying, but if you don't wire that money back here today, I'm gonna get out of my death bed here in this Tulsa hospital and fly out there and kick your ass all over California". Those are the very words he used. He said, "Needless to say, the money was here".

Some of the earliest songs that I learned were songs like "Old Shep" and "The Ballad of Jesse James". When we had our little band, we learned to play some songs in B flat and E flat, and we thought it was cool. I never played an open chord until I got to Nashville – E flat and B flat are good horn chords, and we always had horns in the band.

When I was about sixteen years old in Claremore, I had a friend, Corky Lunsford, who had an uncle named Garr Whitworth who played out near the old KVOO tower on Highway 66. There was a supper club back in there; they could eat and have a mixed drink – of course, the drinks were illegal. Garr would let Corky and me go in there and get back in the corner in a booth; he played the guitar and sang, and his wife played the saxophone and a washtub bass. I'm talking about right after World War II, 1946-45. He would sing the "Pork Chop" song and "Slippin' and Slidin' on My Yass, Yass, Yass". I had never sung those songs in my life until we got to California in 1960, and this club I was working wanted some show songs. We worked up a little show, and I would do those songs. The people started requesting them, so I went to a little studio out there, recorded them, and had a couple thousand cut and sold them at the club. They went real fast.

In 1965, when I moved back to Texas, I had sent some to my brother Chico, and at that time, he was running a little beer joint up on North Memorial in Tulsa, called The Cow Pasture. He was managing it and put it on the juke box. I was back in Odessa when Bill T's Records called and said that they would like to have five hundred copies of it. I sent them and I guess they put them in every beer joint from Tulsa to Arkansas, because I ran into people who would say, "Oh, yeh, you're the guy who sang the 'Pork Chop' and the 'Yass, Yass' songs". Those two songs are the only records I ever put out that featured me singing. The record label that I used when I re-recorded them in Odessa was Pilish Records. At the bottom of the label I put "With Tommy Allsup and the Band, another

Pilish-Hit"; you had to read it slow, and why I did it, I don't know. I thought it was funny, and it was a funny record.

PORK CHOP

Now the other day from out our way, a country boy came to town;

He was all dressed up in his Sunday suit, and he started to mess around.

In his hand he had some pork chops from the best butcher shop in town;

Well, he laid them on the taxi cab seat, and on them a fat lady sat down.

Now the old boy just looked and scratched his head, and here is what he said.

"Well, I don't want it all, I just want some, some of what you're setting on;

Now there ain't no use for us to fuss or fight, we may as well get along.

Now it ain't very neat, but it's there on the seat;

Lady, what you'er setting on is really fine meat.

Now, I don't want it all, I just want some, some of what you're settin' on.

I mean my pork chops, some of what you're settin' on.

I don't know who wrote it, just that Garr Whitworth used to sing it back in the 1940s. He said that he had picked it up probably in the 1930s;

he was pretty old when I learned it from him. The "Yass" song has more verses than I remember.

SLIPPIN' AND SLIDIN' ON MY YASS, YASS, YASS
Tom cat settin' on a sewing machine,
Lickin' his face so he could keep it clean;
Sewing machine sewed so doggone fast,
Sewed twenty-nine stiches 'round his Yass, Yass, Yass.

Same old cat on the mantle piece,
Drug his tail through a pan of hot grease;
Said, "Look out boys, I'm comin' out fast,
A-slippin' and a-slidin' on my Yass, Yass, Yass".

Old Rip Van Winkle slept a mighty long time,
He woke up one morning a-feelin' fine;
He looked around in the tall, tall grass,
Had really long whiskers on his Yass, Yass, Yass.

Ever since I come to this great big nation,
All I ever heard was this confounded "ration;"
They rationed the coffee; they rationed the gas,
I'm glad they didn't ration the ol' Yass, Yass, Yass.

There were a couple other verses that I can't remember. The final verse to "Yass, Yass, Yass" is "If you don't like it, you can kiss my Yass, Yass, Yass".

I always had good singers in my bands, singers who sang better than I did like Little Joe Carson, Bobby Joe Stewart; in Art Davis's band we had Buddy Kendricks and Harold Hitchcock. We always had great singers, so I always led the band and did the arranging; I was always trying to keep the band together. I guess that's why I never did sing, even though I can. I did sing harmony with Buddy and others, but never aspired to be the lead singer. Johnnie Lee used to let me sing, "It's Dark Outside and I'm Scared" and "I'm Not Going Out Tonight". I never did really care about singing; I did it out of necessity.

I've had an excellent life in music; I may have made mistakes here and there, but I'm proud of my contributions to musical America. I guess I can sum up my career with what I learned working for Liberty Records: "Musical hits are made in the studio, not in office committee meetings". And maybe my greatest musical achievement was playing in New York City with Paul McCartney one night and the next night working in Pawhuska, Oklahoma with The Texas Playboys – a contrast in musical styles and locations.

Artists With Whom Tommy Allsup Has Recorded

POP ARTISTS:

Julie London
Andy Williams
Bobby Venton
Edie Gorme & Steve Lawrence
Julie Andrews
Pat Boone
Debbie Boone
Walter Brennan
Mae West
Ernie Freeman
Jack Jones
Martin Denny
Andy Griffith
Johnny Tilleson
Herb Ellis
Tommy Garretts 50 Guitars
Jim Neighbors
Patti Page
Manhattan Transfer
Si Zenter
Al Hirt
Steve Allen
Nick Noble
Brian Hyland
Carol Channing
Bill Medley
Clint Eastwood
Bobby Goldsboro
Andy Griffith
Gomer Pyle (Jim Nabors)
Doc Adams (Milburn Stone)
Festus (Ken Curtis)

ROCK & ROLL AND ROCKABILLY:

Buddy Holly
Bobby Vee
Johnnie Burnette
Gene McDaniels
Timi Yuro
Jan & Dean
The Ventures
Del Shannon
Leon Russell
Jerry Lee Lewis
Troy Shondell
Zager & Evans
Buddy Knox
The Fleetwoods
Screaming Jay Hawkins
Righteous Brothers
Chip Monks
The Crickets
Jack Scott
Bill Haley
Ace Cannon
Norville Felts
Crash Craddock
Bobby Rydell
JackieDeShannon
Eddie Cochran
Jerry Naylor
Charly McClain
Mac Curtis

COUNTRY & WESTERN – Men:
(* Produced by Tommy Allsup)

*Willie Nelson
Waylon Jennings
Kenny Rogers
George Jones
Charley Rich
Johnny Paycheck
Johnny Duncan
Johnny Rodrigues
*Tex Williams
*Bob Wills
Johnnie Lee Wills
*Joe Carson
*Gordon Terry
Statler Brothers
Oak Ridge Boys
Tom T. Hall
Johnny Cash
Rex Allen, Jr.
Bill Anderson
John Anderson
*Asleep at the Wheel
Gene Watson
Moe Bandy
Joe Stampley
Bobby Bare
Ed Bruce
Glen Campbell
Tommy Cash
Roy Clark
David Allen Coe
Little Jimmy Dickens
Everly Brothers
*Mickey Gilley
*Merle Haggard
David Houston
Sonny James

Doug Kershaw
Jimmy C. Newman
Buck Owens
Tommy Overstreet
Carl Perkins
Marty Robbins
Roy Rogers
*Hank Thompson
Mel Tillis
Ernest Tubb
*Slim Whitman
Faron Young
Vince Gill
Steve Wariner
Tim McGraw
Dwight Yokum
Tracy Byrd
Leroy Van Dyke
Cal Smith
Joel Sonyea
Lyle Lovett
Marty Stewart
Merle Travis
Ray Price
Johnny Bush
Johnny Russell
Johnny Rodriquez
Johnny Wright
Johnny Carver
Earl Scruggs Review
*Original Texas Playboys
Bob Luman
*Johnny Lee
David Wills
Con Hunley
Stan Hitchcock

John Wesley Ryles
*Danny Dill
Hugh X. Lewis
Mel Street
Billy Mize &
   Cliff Crofford
The Chipmunks
Hal Willis
Webb Pierce
Marvin Rainwater
Dean Mitchell
Wade Ray
Bowman Brothers
Clay Hart
Wynn Stewart
Augie Meyers
Freddie Hart
Larry Gatlin
Charlie Daniels
Mack Davis
Joe Ely
The McCormick
   Brothers
B. J. Thomas
Del Reeves
Terry Bradshaw
Red Steagall
Gil Prather
Porter Wagner
Buddy Alan Owens
Carl Smith
David Frizell
Jimmy Dean
Johnny Darrell

170

COUNTRY & WESTERN – Women:

Dolly Parton
Tammy Wynette
Lynn Anderson
Karen Kelly
Billie Jo Spears
Jody Miller
Sammy Smith
Crystal Gail
Kitty Wells
Vickie Carr
Shelly West
Tanya Tucker
Dottie West
Connie Smith
Jeannie Pruitt

Stella Parton
Marie Osmond
Barbara Mandrell
Brenda Lee
Wanda Jackson
Dale Evans
Patti Page
Dotsy
Jan Howard
Cristy Lane
Janie Fricky
Billy Jo Spears
Jeanie Seely
Lorrie Morgan
Bonnie Owens

Margo Smith
Barbara Fairchild
Janie Frickie
Mother Maybelle Carter
June Carter
Helen Carter
Anita Carter
Jean Sheppard
Reba McIntyre
Lee Ann Womack
Dixie Chicks
The Kendalls

Some of The Famous Musicians With Whom Tommy Allsup Has Worked and/or Recorded:

Leon McAuliffe
Eldon Shamblin
Jimmy Bryant
Speedy West
Al Hirt
Ernie Freeman
Buddy Emmons
Johnny Gimble
Buddy Spicher
Hargus "Pig" Robbins
Bob Moore
Buddy Harmon
Floyd Cramer
Scotty Moore
James Burton
Glen Campbell
Leon Russell

David Gates
Si Zentner
Herb Ellis
Roy Lanham
Barney Kessell
Hal Blain
Earl Palmer
Red Calender
Shelly Mann
Red Mitchell
Plaz Johnson
Boots Randolph
Charlie McCoy
Lloyd Green
Tommy Jackson
Keith Coleman
Curley Chalker

Tommy Morrell
Bobby Koefer
Earl Scruggs
Spade Cooley
Bobby Bruce
Pete Wade
King Curtis
Noel Boggs
Howard Roberts
Tommy Tedesco

TOMMY ALLSUP DISCOGRAPHY

In 1964 Tommy recorded *The Buddy Holly* Songbook in Norman
Petty's studio in Clovis; it was a fifty-fifty agreement. Petty provided the
studio, and Tommy supplied the musicians. It was released in England
by Decca and in the United States by Reprise. The disc format is rare;
Tommy reissued it on cassette (T. A. Records 0001), and later it was
issued as a cd. Jerry Allison of the original Crickets was the drummer;
Lynn Bailey from Lubbock provided the electric bass rhythm; and Buzz
Cason played the piano. It is an instrumental rendition of the Holly sounds
that Tommy helped create in the studio and on the tours. It was issued as
a cd by Southland Records.

On the cassette the twelve songs are:

Side one:	*Side two:*
"That'll Be The Day",	"Peggy Sue"
"Think It Over",	"It's So Easy"
"Take Your Time",	"Heartbeat"
"Fool's Paradise",	"Oh Boy"
"True Love Ways",	"Rave On"
"Everyday",	"Maybe Baby"

Twisting the Country Classics. Liberty Records LRP 3225

Side One:	*Side Two:*
1. "Kaw-Liga"	7. "San Antonio Rose"
2. "Under the Double Eagle"	8. "Slow Poke"
3. "I'm Moving On"	9. "Cattle Call"
4. "Jambalaya"	10. "Ida Red"
5. "Wildwood Flower"	11. "Sugar Foot Rag"
6. "Wabash Cannon Ball"	12. "Orange Blossom Special"

The Hits of Charley Pride played by Tommy Allsup &
The Nashville Survey. GRT (8 Track)

Program A:	*Program C:*
"One of These Days"	"Does My Ring Hurt Your Finger"
"Lie to Me"	"Let the Chips Fall"
"Let Me Help You Work It Out"	"I Know One (cont.)"

Program B:
"Kaw-Liga"
"The Easy Part's Over Now"
"Just Between You and Me"

Program D:
"I Know One (concl.)"
"The Day the World Stood Still"
"Too Hard to Say I'm Sorry"

The Hits of Tammy Wynette (Tennessee Saxes).
Side One:
1. "Stand By Your Man"
2. "I'll See Him Through"
3. "I Don't Wanna Play House"
4. "Run Woman Run"
5. "Take Me to Your World"
6. "Your Good Girl's Gonna Go Bad"

Side Two:
7. "He Loves Me All the Way"
8. "D-I-V-O-R-C-E"
9. "The Ways to Love a Man"
10. "Apartment #9"
11. "Singing My Song"

Nashville (Tennessee Saxes). Epic KE 32916.
Side One:
1. "A Very Special Love Song"
2. "Pass Me By"
3. "Tie A Yellow Ribbon"
4. "The Most Beautiful Girl"
5. "Paper Roses"
6. "Behind Closed Doors"

Side Two:
7. "Rocky Top"
8. "You Don't Know Me"
9. "Let Me Be There"
10. "Welcome Home"
11. "Orange Blossom Special"

Gospel Guitar Gathering. Living Records LLR-1004 (cassette); recorded and produced by Tommy Allsup Recording Studio, Nashville; Lou Bradley, engineer; Tommy Allsup, guitars; Nashville Sounds, background singers; reissued with songs rearranged (cd) under the title

Gospel Guitar, Konawa Music Productions
Side one:
1. "How Great Thou Art"
2. "Amazing Grace"
3. "Turn Your Radio On"
4. "Peace in the Valley"
5. "Just a Closer Walk with Thee"

Side two:
6. "I'll Fly Away"
7. "Why Me Lord"
8. "The King Is Coming"
9. "One Day at a Time"
10. "Will the Circle Be Unbroken"

10 Great Country Classics. Living Records LLR-1003 (cassette); recorded and produced by Tommy Allsup Recording Studio, Nashville; Lou Bradley, engineer; Tommy Allsup. Guitars; Randy Pandy, drums; Bunky Keel, piano; Dave Martin, bass; Bobbi Seymour, steel guitar; Nashville Sounds, background singers.

Side one:
1. "It Don't Hurt Anymore"
2. "Am I Losing You"
3. "Detroit City"
4. "Sweet Dreams"
5. "Four in the Morning"

Side two:
6. "Hello Walls"
7. "Rose Colored Glasses"
8. "Four Walls"
9. "I Love You Because"
10. "True Love Ways"

AWARDS

Wrangler Award. National Cowboy Hall of Fame and Western Heritage Center, Oklahoma City, Oklahoma, for the Best Western Album, *For the Last Time*, 1975.

Produced the First Western Swing long play album, *For the Last Time*, honored by the Library of Congress, Washington, D. C., 1975.

Inducted into the California Western Swing Hall of Fame, Sacramento, California, 1990.

Inducted into the Texas Western Swing Hall of Fame, San Marcos, Texas, 1995.

Honored by the Oklahoma House of Representatives for Contributions to Country & Western Music, 1998.

Inducted with Bob Wills and The Texas Playboys into the Rock & Roll Hall of Fame, Cleveland, Ohio, 1999.

Inducted into the Canada Rock-A-Billy Hall of Fame, 1999, and the U. S. Rock-A-Billy Hall of Fame.

Grammy Award Country Instrumentalist. With Asleep at the Wheel for "Bob's Breakdown" on their album *Ride with Bob*, February 23, 2000.

Living Legend Award. Native American Music Awards, October 3, 2009.

BIBLIOGRAPHY

Amburn, Ellis. *Buddy Holly: A Biography*. New York: St. Martin's Griffin, 1996.

Griggs, Bill. "February 3, 1959". *Rockin'* (February 1989) 16: 6-14.

Denisoff, R. Serge. *Waylon: A Biography*. Knoxville: University of Tennessee Press, 1983.

Draper, Robert. "The Real Buddy Holly". *Texas Monthly 23* (October 1995) 10: 108-112, 150-155.

Goldrosen, John and Beecher, John. *Remembering Buddy*. New York: De Capo Press, 1996 (revised edition of the 1986 edition and of *Buddy Holly: His Life and Music* [1975] and *The Buddy Holly Story* [1979]).

Jennings, Waylon, with Lenny Kaye. *Waylon: An Autobiography*. New York: Warner Books, 1996.

Kelly, Michael "Doc Rock". *Liberty Records: A History of the Recording Company and Its Stars*, 1955-1971. Jefferson, NC: McFarland & Co., 1993.

Lehmer, Larry. *The Day the Music Died:The Last Tour of Buddy Holly, the "Big Bopper", and Ritchie Valens*. New York: Schirmer Books, 1997.

Opdyke, Steven. *Willie Nelson Sings America*. Austin, TX: Eakin Press, 1998.

Townsend, Charles R. "Homecoming: Reflections on Bob Wills and His Texas Playboys 1915-1973". Los Angeles, CA: United Artists Records, 1974 (Booklet accompanying *Bob Wills and His Texas Playboys: For the Last Time* United Artists UA-LA 216-J2).

Whitburn, Joel. *The Billboard Book of Top 40 Hits*. Rev. & enl. 6th ed. New York: Watson-Guptill Publications, 1996.

Wooley, John. "A Storied Career". *Oklahoma Magazine*. XIV(July 2010) 7: 204, 206.

VIDEOS

The Buddy Holly Story. Culver City, CA: Columbia Pictures, 1978; motion picture starring Gary Busey, et al.

The Real Buddy Holly Story. West Long Branch, NJ: White Star, n. d., produced and hosted by Paul McCartney.

HONKYTONK MAN. Produced and directed by Clint Eastwood; music coordinated by Snuff Garrett; Warner Brothers Entertainment, DVD issue in 2003, WB 27529.

DISCOGRAPHY

This is not intended to be a complete discography of the members of the Winter Dance Tour or of the musicians and entertainers produced by Tommy Allsup or of Tommy's session work; it is merely a sampling of Tommy's activities, experiences and friendships in the music world.

Allsup, Tommy:

Gospel Guitar Gathering. Konawa Music Productions (cassette); Recorded at and Produced by Tommy Allsup Recording Studio, notes by Ken Youngblood; reissued with songs rearranged (cd).

Buddy Holly Songbook featuring the guitar of TOMMY ALLSUP. T. A. Records 0001 (cassette); reissued.

10 Great Country Classics. Konawa Music Productions, Living Records LLR-1003 (cassette); Recorded at and Produced by Tommy Allsup Recording Studio, notes by Ken Youngblood.

Allsup, Tommy and Leon Rausch:

A Tribute to the Music of Bob Wills. Sims Records SRBS-100, 1997 (3 CDs).

Bob Will's: A Tribute to Bob's 100th Birthday. Common Ground Records CGR 7230, 2005. Produced by Tommy Allsup, featuring 21 different artists.

Asleep At the Wheel:

Texas Gold. Capitol Records ST 11441, 1975; produced by Tommy Allsup (12" lp).

Wheelin' and Dealin'. Capitol Records ST 11546, 1976; co-produced by Tommy Allsup, Konawa Music Productions, and Asleep At the Wheel Productions (12" lp).

The Wheel. Capitol Records ST 11620, 1977; co-produced by Tommy Allsup, Konawa Music Productions, and Asleep At the Wheel Productions (12" lp).

Ride with Bob. Dreamworks DRMD 50117, 1999 (cd & cs).

Brennan, Walter. *Old Rivers.* Liberty Records LRP-3233, 1962 (12" lp); produced by Snuff Garrett; reissued by EMI-Capitol Music CCMO027-2 (cd).

Dion and The Belmonts. *The Best of Dion and The Belmonts.* EMI Music Australasia 8141542 (cd).

Holly, Buddy:

The Best of Buddy Holly. Coral Records 7CXSB-8 (2 12" lps).

The Buddy Holly Collection. MCA Records MCAD2-10883 (2 cds).

The Buddy Holly Story. Coral Records CRL 57279 (12" lp).

McWhorter, Frankie:

The Ranch Dance Fiddle: Frankie McWhorter. Produced by Lanny Fiel, Frankie McWhorter, and Tommy Allsup; Fiel Publications FPRS 0005, 1997 (cd).

Texas Sandman. Produced by Lanny Fiel, Frankie McWhorter, and Tommy Allsup; Fiel Publications FPRS 0006, 1999 (cd).

Nelson, Willie. *Willie Neslon: The Early Years.* Liberty Records C2-28077, 1994 (2 cds).

Original Texas Playboys, The. *Live and Kickin'*. Capitol Records ST-11725, 1978; recorded live at Knotts Berry Farm, October 1, 1977 (12" lp).

Richardson, J. P. *Hellooo Baby! The Best of the Big Bopper*, 1954-1959. Rhino Records R2 70164 (cd).

Thompson, Hank:

Back in the Swing of Things. Produced and arranged by Tommy Allsup for Konawa Music Productions; ABC Dot Records DOSD-2060, 1976 (12" lp).

Brand New Hank. ABC Records AY 1095, 1978 (12" lp); Tommy Allsup, bass guitar.

Doin' My Thing. Produced and arranged by Tommy Allsup for Konawa Music Productions; ABC Dot Records DO-2091, 1977 (12" lp).

The Thompson Touch. Produced and arranged by Tommy Allsup for Konawa Music Productions; Dot Records DO-2069, 1977 (12" lp).

Valens, Ritchie. *Come On, Let's Go!*. Del-Fi Records DFBX 2359 (3 cds).

Various Artists. *West Texas Bop*. Ace Records Ltd. CDCHD 699, 24 songs recorded by Norman Petty (cd).

Wills, Bob:

Bob Wills Sings and Plays. Liberty Records LST 7303 (12" lp).

Bob Wills and His Texas Plays: For the Last Time. United Artists Records UALA 2116-J2 (2 12" lps, now available on compact disc).

Bob Wills and His Texas Playboys: In Concert. Produced by Tommy Allsup; Capitol Records SKBB-11550, 1976 (2 12" lps).

Wills, Chill. *Hello, Cousin.* Produced by Tommy Allsup and Bob Hinkle; arranged and conducted by Tommy Allsup; Metromedia Records MD 1017, 1969 (12" lp).

OTHER SOURCES

Interviews with Tommy Allsup:

July 2, 1997; July 3, 1997; July 5, 1997; July 6, 1997; July 8, 1997; September 16, 1997; September 17, 1997; August 12, 2009.

Interviews with siblings at family gatherings were not always recorded.

Interviews with Larry Scott, Snuff Garrett and Carl Bunch.

Attended many shows and dances where Tommy was the leader of the band.